In the famous words of Charles Dickens

"It was the best of times; it was the worst of times."

That pretty much is what your first love is like. Well, maybe any love. Okay maybe life in general. Only having just experienced my first love, I wouldn't know about others. It would be nice to know that it gets better, easier, but I doubt it.

Okay, so it is a first love for three of us, a second love for one. Yet it is so different from her other that it is like a first love. Put in a better way, it is a first "real" love and first relationship beyond that of being just friends.

Also by Rose Weiss

Faith Can Light A Candle In The Dark

A Journey Through The Wilds

Mi Corazon

Published in cooperation with and Distributed by Lulu
Enterprises
www.lulu.com

A
TRUE
TREASURE

By Rose Weiss

Lulu Enterprises
Morrisville, NC

Distributed by Lulu Enterprises
www.lulu.com

ISBN Number 978-0-6151-6536-3
Printed in the USA

FOREWORD

Some names, denoted by an * when they first appear, have been changed to protect the individuals' identity.

The story contained within these pages is based on actual events. They are my views, feelings, and recollections of those events. Others may view them differently from their unique perspective. I am just telling my story as it happened to me.

Well, this part of my story that is. For each life is a never-ending story and we can but tell a tale or two of what has come about so far or fantasize about the future that is yet to be played out.

I wrote this in a different style than most stories are written, but then I am not the ordinary writer, or the ordinary person. For ease, I write in the first person even though it was different alters who experienced these events. It just would be too confusing to do it any other way.

This was not an easy story to tell. It feels far more personal than the poems I have already have published. Be warned that to those who may read this who have experienced traumas it could be triggering. Perhaps too they may find a kind of comfort in knowing that others have been through it and survived. They may find a hope in the sunshine that I found despite all the storms.

I would like to thank my brother, Dante, for believing in me and continuing to encourage me on those darkest of days. I thank my friends near and far, for their patience and understanding. I thank the librarians at Caestecker Library for their encouragement and for creating a very welcoming and comfortable atmosphere so unlike most libraries I have been in. I thank Lulu Enterprises for making all this possible and for the ease of the print-on-demand process through their website. Most of all I would like to thank my muse and constant inspiration, the greatest love of my life and my greatest joy, Jay. I love you with all my heart.

CHAPTER ONE

In the famous words of Charles Dickens, "It was the best of times; it was the worst of times." That pretty much is what your first love is like. Well, maybe any love. Okay maybe just life in general. Only having just experienced my first love, I wouldn't know about others. It would be nice to know that it gets better, easier, but I doubt it. Okay, so it is a first love for three of us, a second love for one. Yet it is so different from her other that it is like a first love. Put in a better way, it is a first "real" love and first relationship beyond that of being just friends.

Before you really get confused, I need to explain something here. I am a multiple. Officially, the disorder is known as, Dissociative Identity Disorder, also called Multiple Personality Disorder. It is quite common actually, though not as understood and accepted as other mental illnesses and disorders. It certainly is interesting to live with.

As for love, well, that gets very interesting too. See any poor fool who chooses to be with me, has to deal with all of me, all of the separate little identities that make up this one Rose. Then there are the other things that go along with it: mood swings, phobias, panic attacks, nightmares, body memories, flashbacks. You get the picture. There are some good things as well. Since each of us is different, it is like having more than one girlfriend without all the sneaking around and lies and jealousy. What guy would not like that!

It adds a new dimension to a relationship doesn't it? As if relationships were not hard enough. It is that mix that keeps everything interesting, though. You appreciate the sweet from experiencing the bitter. The hard struggles either strengthen and cement you together or drive you apart. You can find happiness in the quiet times as well as when there is a lot of excitement and passion. There is comfort in a simple touch, a hug, just in another person's company.

I never thought that I would ever have a boyfriend. I am the kind of girl that is considered nice and sweet and friend material, but not dating or girlfriend material. No way! Well, I do not suppose being real shy helps, or being so damn afraid of everything. I learned very young that the world is not so nice a place and I had to be very quiet and very small, a Nobody, to not attract any attention. Attention to me equaled pain of one kind or another. Well, it is hard to stop doing that when you get to a point where you would like some attention. When you have entered a world different from what you have always known. Okay, a certain kind of attention. Being a wallflower is safe and all, but boring and very lonely.

You could say that for a long time I was repressed or locked away. All of us insiders were. On the outside, the world saw a façade. One of those every girl faces that remind you of someone, though you can never remember who. No one really knew us, but then we didn't even know us. I pretended I was okay being alone, that it did not matter. Well, what else do you do when you don't believe life will ever be any other way? When you have been taught that you aren't of much value and no one really wants to be around you?

Breaking down was a very difficult thing to go through. My world started to shake in small ways. Night terrors - so much fun---NOT!!!! Deep anxiety and fear. It took me six months before I could go farther than my porch when I moved into this one apartment in Beloit. Here I was taking care of other people's kids and I couldn't go to the school plays they were in or just down the block to the pharmacy. One of the few places left that actually had penny candy, for a penny. Imagine that.

How do you explain to a child that you can't go because you are afraid to walk out your front door? It bothered me a lot and I had to do something about it. I found that when I walked with one of the kids that I was fine. Well mostly. My attention was more focused on them, which is what made the difference I think. But if I walked alone, fear set in and I was back home before I got more than 200 feet away. As I ventured out, I was able to go farther and farther from home. Just little steps, little pushes to go a little bit farther. Eventually I was going for early morning walks down by the river to start my day. That I really enjoyed. Though there would still be days when the fear would be too great for me to leave the house, they were fewer.

One of the boys I supervised, Michael*, because he had grown too big for a "babysitter", told me that I had said something that I had absolutely no memory of saying. I thought he was trying to put one over on me, you know, but some of the other kids confirmed it. They also said that it wasn't the first time, either. Well, that shook me up as you can imagine. I know that my childhood for the most part is this big black blank, but to not remember what I had said just the other day or a few hours ago. It was very weird. I could not make any sense of it. Yet there were other things too that I couldn't remember. I had somewhat of a routine so I generally knew what I did each day and kept a record of when the kids were dropped off and picked up. It was specific details I sometimes struggled with of what had happened. My present memory was feeling more and more like the little snippets I had of my past, just postcards of someone else's life. Yet, maybe it was always like this and I had not realized it. None of this might be new at all.

Near the end of that summer of 2001, I moved in with Jake's* family to help them out. Jake lived on the same block and we had become friends. His father was taking an over-the-road type of job and his mother would like someone to help with the house when she wasn't feeling well and to be a sort of companion for her when her husband was away. They seemed like nice people and I had taken care of all their critters once when they were on vacation to Florida, so I agreed.

I had met Jake in 1999 when Michael and another boy I was supervising were running around in the alley near my apartment. Jake was in his back yard with a German Shepherd his family had. I had seen Jake on his paper route at times. But it wasn't until I went into the alley looking for the boys, that I actually met him. He started coming over and hanging with the boys, keeping them out of trouble and playing with the other kids I was watching.

I met Jake's family the night that German Shepherd was hit by a car. What a terrible night! Seems that someone had done it deliberately too. They hit the dog twice. The initial hit, swerving to run directly at him, and then after backing up, they hit him again. Jake came running to get me and I helped as much as I could. I let them use my phone to call the animal hospital. By the time someone actually was there at the hospital to answer the phone, it was too late. The dog passed on while in the van on the way there. Jake was so upset he punched the back out of the mailbox.

Some time after that Jake's sister started to hang over at my apartment too, with some of her friends. So I had teenagers and little ones all at my place. We would play Uno around this big wooden table in my dining room with the kids or Hand and Foot. Hand and Foot is Canasta, but instead of using two decks of cards, you use six. Yeah, I said six. Try shuffling all that. When it was nice out, we would all sit on the porch chatting while the kids played in the yard.

Many people in the neighborhood came to know where to look for their kids when they couldn't find them at home, whether teen or little, because they all hung out at my house. I didn't do anything special. I just treated them like human beings. I talked to them and perhaps more importantly, I listened. Maybe that is why kids have always liked me. Well, and I have always felt more comfortable around kids than adults. With my past who could blame me.

I was considered the "crazy lady" in the neighborhood. I lived like a nun. I had never been married, had no boyfriends, no children of my own. I sometimes put up little signs on my windows about social/political/faith issues. I was heavy into all that at the time. I never pushed my views on anyone though. I did have house rules, but they were for me too. I don't believe in double standards. When someone was in trouble or needed something, I was ready to do what I could. That earned me respect in a neighborhood filled with problems and hatred. I never had problems with the gang bangers or drug dealers, as if everyone knew not to mess with me or was afraid to or something. I mean I never had my apartment broken into or any of the other problems associated with life in the "hood".

I still had no idea what was happening to me. I was living in a façade and fully believed it. I was changing and engaging in the world around me in a different way. Very scary and yet exciting too. It was exciting to start feeling as if I was really living and not just going through the motions. It was scary because it was all so different from the world I knew, from what I thought I knew about myself. I wasn't just doing things I had never done before, but feeling things I had never felt before, never thought I would feel. Things I shouldn't feel from the stand point of who I believed I was, what I believed my life could be like, which added to my fear and anxiety and confusion.

Things went from bad to worse. My world no longer shook a little. It started to crumble and fall apart. First one thing and then another tumbling down like an avalanche. I started having flashbacks, like they talk about with war veterans. Where they go back in their mind to some other place and time and get lost in it so completely it becomes real. They feel like they really are there.

It was in the fall just a few months after I had moved in with Jake's family, November I think. Jake's sister Vicki* had a baby girl, who by then was about 6 months old. Vicky had bought her a high chair and was putting it together in the living room. Just a regular high chair like you would see at Wal-Mart, all made out of heavy plastic with a vinyl cushion. I began to panic and had to run from the room. In fact, I had to run out of the house borrowing Jake's walkman. Music was always something I had enjoyed and turned to when I was upset. I needed it that night, badly.

It was a beautiful night. Stars shining. Weather a little cool but not too cold. A perfect fall evening. I hardly noticed it. My heart was racing a thousand beats a minute. Okay not that fast but it felt like it would beat right out of my chest. I could hardly catch a breath. I wasn't even walking all that fast either. It couldn't have been just from seeing a high chair. I mean that is ridiculous. I had been a babysitter since I was 11 years old. I had seen plenty of high chairs.

After getting back, Jake and his mom, Esther*, were there. I sat down on the couch. Then I just reached out and grabbed Jake's hand as he walked past me. Esther, who was in school at the time studying for a degree in family counseling, went into therapist mode. She began asking me questions about what was going on, what I was feeling.

Jake sat down on the other couch (the two were in an L shape) and began to gently stroke the back of my hand with his thumb. Good thing too, for it kept me grounded.

In my mind, I started going back to some other place, some other time. At first the picture was hazy, just shadows. It never got completely clear but clear enough to see what was happening. With the images came a flood of emotions and physical sensations.

I was in an apartment that I did not recognize. Bright sunlight was pouring in through the windows along with a breeze that was cool, chilling me. I saw the shadow of a woman with long hair moving around the room. I could hear leaves rustling in the breeze. Then some man came in through the front door. He had forced his way in. The woman started yelling and fighting him. I felt a deep affection towards her and grew afraid. There was a sensation on my cheek, a sting with warmth, like I had been cut by something. *(Afterwards, talking with Jake and his mom, they said that a mark appeared on my left cheek and then slowly disappeared again. Freaky huh?)* Then I felt these huge hands on me holding me down so I could not move. I was very scared now, shaking, and so cold. I was being held down in the chair I was in. It was a high chair! I could feel the sides of it. I was just a baby! Then, the images were gone and I was back on the couch in Jake's living room.

Jake went and got my blanket for me and tucked it around my legs. It was a knit blanket with red stripes alternating with white stripes that had ladybugs down them. It was like a security blanket for me when I was having a rough time. I felt like an icicle. It took a while to warm up and the shaking to stop. I had never experienced anything like that before. It was like having a nightmare when you are fully awake. No, it is worse than a nightmare. Nightmares you know you will wake up from. This, I had no idea when I would come out of it or when it would happen again, or where.

Like a dam breaking open and the water pouring out, with that one flashback a torrent was released in me. All I thought I knew would be stripped away. I would be fine and then boom, another wave of emotion or a deep depression would descend. I was afraid most of the time. My behavior was strange and erratic. I felt like I was not even myself anymore. My voice, my walk, my expressions, my reactions to people and things would just change at times. Even how I reacted to Jake and our friendship would radically change at times, confusing me. Words would just pop out of my mouth. I would get angry and snap. *(I was normally even tempered.)* Maybe there was more going on than just PTSD (Post Traumatic Stress Disorder), but I would not find out for sure what until Jake, his parents, and I all moved up to central Wisconsin. Though there were clues of course. There are always clues.

Jake was my only friend. In fact, he was the first real friend that I had had in a very long time. He became the one I turned to and leaned on when things got bad. When I was afraid, scared out of my mind, and couldn't come out of my room, he was the only one I felt safe with, trusted. He was there for me. He gave me my first non-little kid hug and held me when I was trembling until I calmed. He helped with my bouts of depression by making a little joke or a funny face, which made me smile, or by sitting with me listening to music or watching a movie. He let me borrow his CDs whenever I needed to. There were some songs that were a great comfort to me or helped me express something I was feeling. They did the same for him.

Jake had had a traumatic past himself. He had been severely abused by a family member. Not to mention being very sick and weak for the first two years of his life. There were things that he had experienced that he could talk to no

14

one about. Things that no one believed, like his ability to see auras and spirits, or how when as a small child he could enter his mother's dreams, even nightmares. Things that no one else in the family wanted to think about or deal with. Jake's uncle stealing from them that was okay to mention, but his abuses towards Jake and his sister…no way. To joke around about Jake's grandfather haunting the house, that was okay, but not the female who haunted Jake's room and made him afraid of me after I moved in.

When Jake first told me about something he had experienced, I believed him. I think I was the first one who ever really did, maybe the only one. That was when we started to become friends, him seeing that I did believe him and understood. He often stopped by for a few minutes to chat while finishing up his paper route. He would "escape" to my apartment when something was going on at home or to avoid chores. Come on, who could blame him. What teenager likes doing chores, especially dishes?

Moving up north turned out to be great for Jake. He started making new friends and feeling better about himself. Being the new guy in town, he could sort of revamp himself. He didn't have to worry about people teasing him because of how he used to look or act when younger. It was all based on how he looked and acted now. The confidence he had finally found and the weight he had lost. He looked good and carried himself straighter, prouder, not vain-like pride, but more comfortable with himself. He still struggled with low self-esteem of course and just wanted to be liked, to belong.

Meanwhile, I could barely come out of my room and was very scared and well, a basket case. Everything was new and strange and I leaned on him too much. I became too dependent on him, on his strength, on his friendship. I would sometimes get mad and jealous that he didn't want to be my friend any more and would rather be with all these new friends. Who could blame him? I wasn't the same person anymore. I didn't like being around me half the time, maybe more than half the time.

I started to really crash, a major breakdown. First, it was the nightmares and panic attacks, general fear. Then one day a motor cycle went by and I had a panic attack worse than any I had had before. I ran up to my room.

If you have never had a panic attack, count yourself lucky. It is horrible to experience. You start having trouble breathing, taking more and more breathes trying to get air into your lungs, until you are hyperventilating. Your chest begins to hurt, like you are having a heart attack. You shake all over. You get cold even on the warmest of days. It feels like someone put you on a wild carnival ride. There is an overwhelming need to run, to flee, just go somewhere anywhere, but where you are. Of course not all panic attacks are that severe, but when they are, oh boy!

When I thought I had calmed down, my head started feeling all funny, like it was numb. I was wobbly going to the stairs but I needed to find Jake, someone. I fell on the stairs, my legs just going out from under me, tumbling down a few steps. Thank God, they were carpeted. I ended up going down the rest of the way on my bottom. I was not going to chance falling again.

I called and called but Jake wasn't around. I was all alone in the house. I crawled back up the stairs. I managed to get to my feet holding onto the railing for support. I was still very wobbly. Then in my room, my legs fell out from under me again and I landed on the floor just beside my bed. I was so scared. I put my headphones on and cranked it up, thinking that this feeling would soon pass. I was wrong.

Another flashback swept me up. This time there was not much in the way of clear images, just shadows. It was mostly sounds and physical sensations. The music from my CD player sounded like it was coming from a distance, even though the headphones were still firmly on my ears. I didn't

16

even know when the music had stopped playing. The sound was so far away. The other flashback was tame compared to this one. Afterwards I just lay there curled in a ball, not able to get up. I did not want anything but the pain to go away. I looked at my hand and was surprised by its size. I asked myself, why I had a woman's hand. It didn't feel like my hand at all, but some stranger's hand.

I was so tired and in so much pain, physical as well as emotional. I just wanted it to end to go away. I just wanted to give up. Then I heard this voice whisper in my ear, "Breathe." I had stopped breathing. I turned the music back on. Its steady, strong, hard rock rhythm kept my heart beating and my lungs drawing in air. In my mind began to run images, memories of my friendship with Jake and I felt the strength to fight on build in me.

All the rest of that day, all that night, and into the next day, I lay on the floor with my comforter over me. No one checked on me. I could have sworn that when the flashback was coming and I had fallen to the floor of my room that I was screaming, just screaming for help. That I screamed during the flashback. How could no one hear me? Or was it just that they didn't care? It wasn't like I lived alone. Jake's room was right next to mine. He must have seen me lying on the floor through my open doorway. Didn't he? Is it any wonder I felt alone and uncared for, abandoned, and just wanted to give up? Who wouldn't?

By then I was able to move enough to crawl up onto my bed. Good thing my mattress and box spring were on the floor at the time. There I stayed sleeping for another day or two. I am not sure. Time was lost and I lost in it.

When Jake finally ventured in to check on me, what he saw.... I was a mess. I was so weak he had to help me down the stairs. Then he sat me down at the table and insisted I eat something. Esther was there too at the computer, which was kept in the dining room. She was surprised by my condition. I had spent several days in my room before, many times in fact. Never had I come out looking like this. I could only eat part of the bowl of applesauce Jake placed in front of me. It was all I could manage. Then I went back upstairs and went to sleep. I was so very tired.

The next day I went downstairs, feeling a little stronger, to take a shower. I sure needed one. Gross!!! I looked in the mirror, at my image. Oh my God! I looked all grey and pasty, like I hadn't eaten in two weeks. My cheeks were sunken in. Dark circles colored the skin under my eyes. I looked like one of the walking dead, a zombie.

That flashback is what brought out Lolo, a little 3 year old. It was what had happened to her. No wonder I was surprised by the size of my hand. I was a multiple and was looking at my hand with the eyes of that 3 year old!

To aid in getting my strength back, Jake brought to me a little kitten who was also weak and needed TLC. The kitten and I took care of each other. Jake watched over both of us. I named her Sassy, which suited her perfectly. Sometimes Lolo came out and would play and laugh. It was weird of course, but it also felt more real and natural.

However, things did not stay good. The Fourth of July arrived. All the noise from the fireworks going off around town was terrifying me. I love fireworks, so why were they now scaring me so bad I would jump and scream? I was getting terrible headaches too. Jake suffers from migraines and let me take one of his pills. Boy! Did that work good. Not just numbed the pain, but I could sleep. Just complete zone out. Wonderful!

That turned into a problem as the wave of emotions got worse and fear increased to an unbearable degree. The house was full of people. Jake's sister Vicky, with her boyfriend, was there. She was heavily pregnant with her second child and couldn't work anymore. She needed to be on bed rest so she didn't deliver early. They were going to

18

be moving in with us. Also with Vicky was Sally*, a girl who was Jake's best friend back in Beloit. I had a problem with her. See before we moved, Sally had started teasing me. She was saying nasty things about my friendship with Jake as well as comments about what I was going through. She said I was faking and making it all up for attention. Please. Whatever. As if I wasn't under enough stress here's some more. Congratulations! Yeah, thanks God. Thanks a lot.

I was staying upstairs most of the time. There was a little sitting area where I had my loveseat and two chairs. Our bedrooms, mine and Jake's that is, were off of this. There were two other bedrooms downstairs off the living room, one was his parent's room and the other was where his niece stayed when she was up visiting.

I was bad, very bad. I was not eating. I wasn't hungry and the headaches were bad so I couldn't eat much anyways. I was taking Jake's migraine medicine, more often than directed to on the label and more than one pill at a time. Sometimes I would mix it with Esther's migraine medication. It was a different prescription. These were no light medicines either but some of the strongest migraine medicines available at the time. What I was doing was very dangerous. So why do it? I just wanted to numb out, to zone. With the pills and the headphones, I could drive out the rest of the world. I did not hear the fireworks so I did not jump and scream with terror. I did not hear the noise of the house full of people. I did not hear any motorcycles go by. I was off in my own little world.

It was to be just temporary until the 4th of July was over and things calmed down. I think Jake knew I was not eating and was sleeping all the time. I think he knew about the pills too, but he didn't say anything.

Something snapped in me. I spiraled down into a deep depression. I mean way, way down. I was already depressed of course. I didn't think at this time I was ever not depressed to some extent. I had been deep before, feeling I was being pulled downwards by these hands clawing at me through the floor. It really felt like hands too and I could not break their grip. I could sense this dark pit of blackness below me. Jake heard me and picked me up off the floor. That was like rising up on eagle's wings to safety. Anyways, I was going deep again. This time no hands clawed dragging me down, just despair. I felt alone, abandoned, unloved, and unwanted. I was just a worthless body of flesh that was only here to be hurt and used and tossed aside and no one cared.

What I didn't explain earlier, with the flashback, was the nature of the memory. I think you need to understand just how horrible that memory was to understand why I was in such a bad state. You see when I was 3, well… This is not easy to tell. It is so horrible. There was a man who rode a Harley Davidson motorcycle, who was one of the many lovers of my mother. (*Thank God, she isn't really my mother and yet, she was. Since she was the one who was to raise and care for me, be my mother, after my biological mother was killed and she was the only mother I had known.*) I was drugged or something was done to me so I could not move, hence the numbness in my head. Often her and her lovers were drunk or high or some combination of both. It was then that they abused me. Sometimes giving me alcohol or some drug to make it so I didn't struggle didn't scream. Perhaps it lessened the physical injuries to my body too, but not the injury to my mind, my psyche. This man then raped and sodomized me. I actually could feel him flipping over my limp little body from lying on my back to my stomach.

Yeah, I said it was horrible. Can you see now why I zoned out with migraine medication? How do you live with something like that? Not just know that it happened, but relive it, experience it again in all its terror and pain, hearing his voice saying things as he…I mean I was only 3 years old, 3, a baby practically. How could anyone do that to a baby? I couldn't tell anyone about it, no one. It all lay inside of me, churning away at me, beating me down bit by bit on top of everything else.

I went into the little box where I kept all my tools, took out one of my little blades for a utility type knife and I put the edge to my arm. I just wanted to cut, to bleed. I wasn't thinking of suicide. I did not want to die. I just wanted the pain to go away. I felt the sting of the blade and for a second it was sharper than the other pain. I cried and was whispering stuff to my self as I took the blade to my arm again and again. It stopped working. The sting of the blade was no longer good enough. There wasn't even any blood, just angry red scratches. I couldn't even bleed the pain away.

I put the blade back into the box and tried to zone, but that wasn't working either. I laid there on my loveseat with the music playing in my ears watching night slowly pass through the window. Then at dawn, I got up and took a shower. While I was getting dressed, Jake walked in on me and saw the cuts on my arm. When I came out of the bathroom, he was rocking back and forth on the couch in the living room. He did not say anything. He did not even look at me. Maybe I was mistaken about him seeing my arm. Maybe he just had to pee badly. Maybe he was embarrassed by walking in on me and seeing me in my bra. Maybe that was why he was rocking.

I went back upstairs. I had written a note the night before to Jake and hung it up on the wall between our doors, where there was this little corkboard. I don't remember what it said. I was in such a state it could have said anything. I took off the angel necklace, which had been a gift I had received the prior Christmas, and hung it up next to the note. I walked downstairs and out the door into the early morning. I did not even stop to put shoes on. Barefoot, I walked down the sidewalk towards the river. I went and sat for a while at the edge of the water near an old steel bridge.

It was one of those old railroad type bridges with heavy steel crossbeams. It was made to be able to be turned, spun. Why that would be needed across a shallow river, I do not know. Perhaps it used to span part of a bigger river and when that bridge was redone parts were sold off. This section then ended up across a river in Princeton, Wisconsin. It is an interesting mystery. Or maybe not.

I sat upon a slight incline by the waters edge, watching the current flow past me. The sunlight sparkled on the water. It warmed the silk of my long sleeved blouse. It was blue my favorite color, comfortable, and hid the scratches on my arm. I wanted the current to carry me away. But where would I go? To what? It was a nice peaceful spot. Nature usually did have the ability to calm me, quiet my restless spirit, my aching heart.

As the sun rose higher, I grew tired of sitting and started walking again. There was no sidewalk here so I walked on gravel or on tough grass beside the road. I just walked and walked. I had no destination in mind. Just walk until I could walk no more. Maybe disappear into the horizon. Walk until the pain went away, until I went away and could be hurt no more.

I don't know what time it was when I felt like I wanted to go back, to go "home", was ready to go home. As I got closer to the part of town where the house was, Vicky's boyfriend saw me. He said the police were looking for me. That scared me. I mean, why? What had I done? I almost turned tail and ran back the other way. Then I thought, maybe he was just saying that because he didn't like me much. He was that kind of guy, not a very nice person at all.

I reached our block and the police were there. The car pulled over to the side of the road and the officer stopped me. I have always been afraid of men and given what I had recently remembered and that this was a big man, I was terrified. I started to shake. He told me that Jake had called the police after he read the note and could not find me. *(Then Jake must have been out looking for me. He did care. He was worried about me. But why didn't he find me? I hadn't gone all that far.)* I told the officer I was okay and just wanted to go home, but he wouldn't let me.

Esther came down the sidewalk to where I was standing. I had switched. Lolo had come out, and I was crying, so scared, and just kept saying, "I want to go home." Esther happens to be multiple also, so she understood. She was the first one to recognize what was going on inside me, to recognize the signs that indicated I might have DID. *(Although later, she would deny this and accuse me of faking it. Why do these things happen to me?)*

It triggered one of her littles to come out. We were both sitting there on the sidewalk, little girls crying in each other's arms. I did not understand why I couldn't just go home. It was right there. I could see the house. I could see Vicki and her boyfriend and Sally standing there in the yard with Jake's dad, James*. The officer told me I was going to the hospital. I told him, "No way. I don't like hospitals. Please, don't make me go. I just want to go home." Esther said I had to, just for a few days, and then I could come home. She would come see me and we would drink orange sodas together. That was her favorite. The favorite of the alter that was out that is. Her main personality hated orange juice.

To make it worse, as if this wasn't all bad enough, they handcuffed me. Yup. Not the behind the back simple handcuffs either. Nope. This had a thing that went around my waist and then my hands were cuffed together in the front. The officer put this on me right in front of all the neighbors, as if I was some criminal. The officer said he had to, though he didn't want to. It was because he felt I was a danger to myself. With what? I didn't even have shoes on for crying out loud. How could I hurt myself?

I cried all the way from Princeton to Green Lake. I didn't even know where I was going, to which hospital. The officer said we had to stop at the sheriff's department to pick up a female officer. Whatever. I had to wait in that hot car all squished up for an hour, which felt like an eternity. Just sit there all alone, in handcuffs, crying till I didn't think I could cry no more. Discovering I was wrong when the tears came streaming out again. Being stared at by anyone who walked by, wondering what I had done to be there.

It was a long ride to Fond du Lac, where the hospital was. I had no idea what awaited me there, if I would ever get to go home again. The two police officers chatted and had the radio on. I was in hell and they were having a good time. Great!

I arrived at the hospital and, still in those handcuffs, was taken up to the psychiatric floor. A nurse had me sit in one of the chairs in this little lounge area. She looked at my arm and saw that it was only scratches. They weren't even all that red anymore. I am a fast healer. They didn't even need to be cleaned. After I filled out a bunch of paperwork, I was shown around.

There was a guy who was walking with someone down the hall. He looked at me and commented to his friend that she was pretty. He meant me. ME! I mean that isn't something that I hear all that often, hardly ever in fact, and usually by some female who is just trying to make me feel better. I have always felt ugly, still do sometimes. You know, even though I didn't believe him and wondered what medication he was on, hearing it made me feel good. Well, that and the fact that he kept looking at me and came up and talked to me, distracting me from the whole I am in the hospital thing. He ended up being the first guy to ever ask me out. I said no of course. Not that he wasn't a nice guy, he was, even if a bit overwhelming. I just wasn't ready and

24

didn't really believe that he liked me, that anyone could. Plus, there's the whole also a mental patient thing. The hospital is not a good place to start a healthy relationship.

Each day I felt a little bit better. I talked to people, hung out in the lounge or in the dining room. I went to classes and had therapy with a nurse. I didn't like the staff psychiatrist much. Why is it that so many doctors think they know it all and you are just stupid? It is like you aren't even a person to them, just a body, or in my case a crazy mixed up mind. The doctor I saw when I first got to the hospital was nice, though. He was filling in for the regular psychiatrist that weekend. He listened and made suggestions, but let me decide. The other doctor though....You would get more warmth from a brick wall in January.

I called home collect. It is the only way you can call home from the hospital, unless you have a calling card. I talked to Esther. She is one of those people that sees a creature in need and wants to help them. That is why she ended up with so many animals. She just couldn't turn them away. I guess I was like that for her. I had moved in with them to help them out. Now that I was falling apart, she was helping me. Though I know it must not have been easy, dealing with it all, I sure did appreciate it.

I wore scrubs a lot. Those are the outfits you see doctors wearing, particularly surgeons on TV shows. They are very comfortable. The staff had given me a pair of those funny sock/slipper things for my feet, since I didn't have shoes. I only had the one outfit and I couldn't wear that all the time or sleep in it. I was able to wash it though. There was a washer and dryer for patient use. That was nice. Esther didn't have money for gas to come up all that way to see me, so I didn't get more clothes until the day before I was released. My suitcase had been packed with a hodge-podge of things that mostly didn't even go together and no bras or panties. I didn't know who packed it. But it is the thought that counts right? And still no shoes.

The next big thing was I had to stand up in front of a judge before I could be released and go home. Talk about scary. I mean I didn't do anything wrong. Well, not really, not that kind of wrong. Esther and James were there at the courthouse, which helped some. That is where they gave me my suitcase. A lady patient in the hospital let me borrow her shoes. The woman who would be my therapist when I got out was there. Lynn* was a Court Advocate as well as head of the Mental Health Department of the county Social Services.

The courtroom was dark and dreary. Or maybe it felt that way because I was so scared. The judge sat up at this bench. I had to sit at a table on a hard chair. Esther and James sat near by. The Court Advocate sat at the other table with someone else. I did not know what to expect. I had seen courtroom stuff on TV of course, but it is different when you are in the courtroom for real and it's about you.

The police had gone through my journal and the poetry I had written and made copies, all without my permission. Talk about invasion of privacy! The judge asked me questions about it. I explained that I was just expressing how I felt. I did not want to die. I just wanted the pain to stop. Writing helped me to release my feelings. I really hadn't run away or intended to. I just needed to go for a walk.

I had to promise to be a good little girl and go to therapy and take my meds and eat right for 90 days or I would end up in some hospital or somewhere for 6 months. No way, man, was I going to let that happen. This experience was bad enough thank you very much. Though I mean, I was finally getting the help I needed, which is a good thing. I met some real nice people, another good thing. It is just not something I want to repeat, ever.

I was looking forward to getting home. I knew Jake would be mad at me. I couldn't blame him. I would be mad and frustrated and scared and all that too. I never expected…I mean everything had changed. Jake didn't talk to me. I was moved to the downstairs room where Jake's niece usually stayed. My stuff had all been jammed into a closet upstairs and I had to bring it down. It was so that they could keep a better "eye" on me. Okay, I understood that. But all they had moved was my bed. I had wanted to talk to everyone, to explain things as well as I could, but I never did. They all acted like they just wanted to forget it ever happened. I guess I couldn't blame them really. It was intense for everyone. Sally ended up going home right after I left for the hospital. She just couldn't deal with it all.

I tried apologizing to Jake. It was major what had happened to me. I think he felt a little responsible, because he knew I was in trouble and didn't do anything. It could very well have turned out differently and he knew that. I knew it too. I could have died. I probably should have with what I was doing with the meds and all. If I had used a different blade, different kinds of cuts… well you get the idea.

Jake was mad for a long time. He didn't want anything to do with me. It was more than having to be hospitalized. It was how much I had changed. I was no longer the person that he had known. All these alters were coming out. My moods were up and down, in and out, all over the place. It was hard to know what would happen next, who I would be, what would upset me and send me in tears to my room.

Two weeks after coming home from the hospital we had to move. It was just a few blocks away next to a Catholic Church. A friend of Jake's, Todd* and Todd's brother and dad helped us move everything. Todd was the only one to really talk to me, to ask me why I had done what I did. Todd helped me pack up the kitchen, which got him a lot of teasing from the other guys. Why? He was just being helpful. Todd showed me some card tricks to keep me calm while a load was being taken over and we were waiting for them to get back. Jake didn't like it, the attention Todd was giving to me. He looked so angry. I know Todd was like Jake's best friend, but what, he was supposed to ignore me?

All the things I was going through triggered Jake in a way too, triggered his own nightmares, fears, ect. Well that and the alcohol. He had started drinking before we moved north. It made him mean and angry sometimes. He would get so angry even when I didn't do anything wrong. I think he was frustrated too. Here all these things were happening to me and he didn't know what to do or not do. As if being a teenager wasn't hard enough and didn't carry enough problems, let's add to the plate.

Maybe that was why he was angry. But it wasn't my fault all this was happening to me. I didn't ask for it, not one bit of it. I wanted it all to just go away and be like it was before. I didn't like any of this. I mean it was horrible and exhausting and I was just as scared and confused as everyone else, if not more so.

The new house was smaller than what we had been living in. There were only three bedrooms. Jake's parents were on the first floor in a room off the living room. Jake had his own room on the second floor. Vicki, her boyfriend, and her daughter all shared the other second floor bedroom. I was made a room on the back porch.

It was good in one sense because I could go out for walks when I needed to without disturbing anyone, even in the middle of the night. I got into the habit of walking in the cemetery next to the church. It was quiet and I could cry and talk and just sit looking up at the stars without anyone looking at me or making comments. Even in the middle of the night it wasn't scary, just peaceful.

I also spend a lot of time outside on the swing in the backyard. It was a bench swing with a canopy over it. I would sit there reading, or laying down. It was there that I created the inner safe house for the emerging alters. I liked being outside. It helped so much, feeling the sunshine, being out in the rain. Just like when I was little. The outdoors was the only comfort I had back then. So it was becoming again.

There were bad parts to having your room on the back porch. I could be locked out the house, but I couldn't lock the door to the outside. That really played on my feeling like an outcast as well as my vulnerability and fear of strangers. The basement door was just a couple of feet from the end of my bed. I hate basements. There was little to no privacy. There was an interior window looking into the kitchen/dining room, with little kitchen drapes. The dogs and people had to come in and out through my room. I know that it was the only place they could put me. But like I said it played on my feelings of being an outcast, an obligating burden, especially since I couldn't help out with the cooking and cleaning like I used to. But I had no money of my own. I had no other place to go.

CHAPTER TWO

After one month or so in that second house in Princeton, we all moved to Berlin. I hate moving. I mean I really hate it. I have moved too many times for me to even count. I dream of one day having a little cottage of my own so I don't have to move anymore. Being able to be free to decorate any way I want to, would be great, a bonus. Not having to move again…priceless.

I didn't want to be too dependent on anyone, especially not Jake. I had leaned on him way too much. But then he was the first one to ever show me real kindness, tenderness, warmth, to look at me and see a real person. Like a man in the desert dying of thirst, I lapped up that water. I looked for it when I was sinking deep and when I was crawling my way back up. I had been only hated for so very long, I needed to be loved, but was afraid I couldn't be.

Asking and getting help from others when I was struggling was hard for me. I was always the one who helped others. I wasn't allowed to even admit that I might need help, that I couldn't handle it all on my own. It was real hard to put myself first in any way, even if it meant for my health or sanity.

I was in therapy, seeing Lynn about once a week, but I wasn't really doing that much better. I was having a lot of headaches and problems eating, problems sleeping. A lot of problems period. I didn't understand what was going on, why I was sick all the time. I spent more time in bed than out of it, reading or resting. I cooked and cleaned as much as I could, but rarely ate. I was tired all the time, confused all the time. Felt not understood a lot of the time. Then there's the guilt, because I couldn't handle everything, take care of it all, didn't know what was happening to me or why, not really.

It didn't help that Jake's attitude towards me kept shifting. I didn't know what to think, how to react. One minute we would be friends and at times like brother and sister. The next he would be angry and cold and hate me. I guess I was the same way with him, if I think about it. It was a chaotic time for both of us and we took it out on each other.

More alters had emerged. And then there were four: Lolo - 3, Cera -16, Red - 18, and Auntie -23.

Lolo thought of Jake as her big brother and called him JJ. She loved to play with Jake's niece. The two of them were thick as thieves and would sometimes get into mischief, but always a good kind.

One day her and Lolo were there at the house with Jake, everyone else had gone shopping or something. *(We were still living in Princeton at the time.)* Jake was sitting in the recliner watching them as they laid on the floor coloring. Jake knew Lolo was out and was a little mad at having to baby-sit instead of being able to go run around with his friends. Well, he feel asleep. Not wise. They started taking handfuls of crayons and tossing them up in the air quietly giggling as they watched them rain all over the living room. One hit Jake and he jumped up, yelled at them, and stomped out of the house like a bull. I mean if he had been any angrier steam would have come out of his nostrils. Lolo got real upset of course and began to cry. Auntie came out and helped Jake's niece clean up all the crayons and took her outside for a while.

Boy, did Auntie give Jake an earful when she saw him for scaring Lolo like that and making her cry. He apologized, but that dark side of him really scared Lolo and she stayed away from him whenever she noticed that blackness in his eyes. A blackness that I had encountered before, when he was angry, or when he was drinking. A dark, cold blackness that was different from how Jake usually was; harsh and cruel and empty of human warmth or understanding or caring, like a Jekyll and Hyde kind of thing.

Cera was "born" back in Beloit. She was the one whose feelings and view of Jake I had felt and was scared and confused by at the time. When I had met him, he was just the paper boy, a nice kid from the neighborhood. Then one day he was attractive and sweet and all that. I mean it would shake you up too when you are used to living like a nun and don't respond to males like females usually do. When you are generally afraid of all adult males. When you are living under this façade and act like an old woman, dress like an old woman, are viewed by others as an old woman, even if in fact you are not an old woman at all.

For several months, Jake had been broken up with a girlfriend that treated him badly, very badly. During that time, he and Cera hung out a lot. To see them together was like seeing two normal teenagers crushing on each other. He would think of excuses to hold her hand, like to warm them up. They would sit next to each other on the couch whispering about stuff while watching a movie. They would take his telescope out to look at the stars or watch meteors. They looked so cute together. His self-esteem was boosted way up. He would come home from school with this huge bright smile on his face, eager to see her and tell her about his day. She really fell for him and it hurt her when he went back to his girlfriend. But that was also after Sally started teasing and making rude remarks about their friendship and she wasn't the only one either. Something very innocent was twisted in perverted minds to be something else.

Cera didn't make herself "known" though until we were in Princeton. She made friends with Todd's girlfriend and would run off downtown to hang out. She started taking Jake's niece for long walks in the evening in her stroller. It helped his niece calm down and get ready for bed and she often fell asleep before they got back home. It was also a way for me to get out, get some exercise. Quite clever isn't she?

Red revealed herself to me and then went back inside. She appeared in my mind's eye in this long red silky nightgown. She had red hair too, but it was because of that nightgown she was named Red by Lolo and it stayed. As you can probably guess, she is my romantic, and bearer of my sensuality, sexuality, femininity. I was way not ready at the time to deal with those issues and things so Red went back inside till a later date. Though I do think, sometimes she did come out and flirt a little bit with Todd and Jake too, when he wasn't in his black mood that is.

Auntie, that is me. I am the writer, the inner therapist, the caretaker, the mystery solver, the investigator, the "nun". I am now called Tia, which is Spanish for aunt. I am the one who kept up the façade for so long. I thought of myself as an "Aunt" to the little kids I took care of. Some of them even called me aunt.

I know earlier I said my age was 23. Truth be told I am only 13. I stopped aging when the façade was cemented into place. There was an incident I remembered and recorded in my journals, when I started really breaking apart in 2001, that happened shortly after my 13th birthday.

I was walking on the gravel driveway of a farm we were living on in Elkhorn. I often spent my days walking and exploring the farm, which was empty except for three horses that we bordered from the neighbor's farm in one of the pastures. This particular day as I walked, I was overwhelmed by a heaviness of emotion that drove me to my knees. I didn't feel the gravel dig into my skin. I didn't feel anything but this pressure, like a great weight on my shoulders and back holding me down. I felt myself giving up, going away. Although I still breathed and moved and went through all the motions of living after that, I had stopped living. Part of me died that day, just stopped, not to be awakened back to life until so many years later in Beloit. No wonder I was such a mess.

The mother of a friend of mine, some months later after moving again, told me that I looked 30. She actually mistook me for my own mother! What a nice thing to hear huh. I have looked 30 ever since and 30 to a girl of 13 is an old woman. I suppose it was safer to be old. Safe from being hurt anymore. Safe from being at least physically abused by my mother. Though there are far worse abuses than being beaten, that do far greater damage.

Now you can understand, I think, all the confusion that was caused by Cera with regards to Jake. As far as I was concerned and anyone else was concerned I was a 30 year old woman. Okay to be neighborly friends, but best friends and to be crushing, well, that was a problem. Even after it was obvious that I was a multiple it stayed a problem. Jake and his family just couldn't let go of what they thought I was, who they thought I was, what they wanted and needed me to be. For a long time I had tried to live that way, according to what other people wanted, expected, needed. I couldn't any longer. Not totally. I still do in some ways though. It is a constant struggle.

Time passed in Berlin. I was on medication for the depression. I met with my therapist, though it became more sporadic as I had difficulty getting a ride to Lynn's office. I managed to get out sometimes when I was feeling well. I went for long walks. I socialized with Jake and his family. We were starting to become friends again, or at least friendly, at times. Cera was trying to get over her romantic feelings for him and was doing a good job most of the time. She was content just to be friends with Jake, though it was nothing like it had been. The jealousy she felt when he started dating some girl at school was not because she wanted to date him but just wanted to date, to have a boyfriend, to be liked, to be normal. She wanted to go out, make friends, and have fun, instead of stuck around the house all day, every day. Just like a typical teenager. It tore her up when Jake got used and tossed aside by these girls.

What made it harder for Cera was a connection or bond she felt to Jake, a psychic kind of connection. She sensed him, felt what he felt, just knew things that were going on with him, knew when he was in trouble. It was an ongoing feeling. Ever before if I, or some part of me, felt what someone else was feeling or that they were in trouble it was just the once and passed. It wasn't like that with Jake. It was different and attached her to him like to no one else.

Jake felt me too, had felt just by touching my hand what I was feeling inside. Back in Beloit when I was feeling so much pain, he took my hands once to warm them. He was knocked onto the couch by the intensity of my pain and emotions. I mean literally knocked off his feet and had to lie down for a while. That was what I was carrying around inside of me. And that was at the beginning stages of my breaking. Can you imagine how intense it became after the memories started really coming back? How intense when I was crashing and ended up in the hospital? No wonder Jake had to distance himself. No wonder it triggered his own pain. No wonder he had to deny everything, to keep him from feeling and facing his own inner demons.

I quit taking the antidepressants after being on them for 7 months. I am not sure if they ever really worked like they were supposed to. I told my psychiatrist that I was having a problem feeling sick all the time and was having a lot of headaches. His response was to up the medication dose. I tried it for a few weeks, but the numbing out and feeling sick and inability to function, to engage in life got worse. I decided to quit taking them and I stopped seeing that psychiatrist. Not just because of the medication problem, either. I mean that kind of thing is normal isn't it? But see I had another problem with him.

At my last appointment with him, he asked me if I had a boyfriend. When I said no, he asked me if I was a lesbian. I told him no, that guys just don't like me. Then this doctor said, "Why? Are you a snob?" That really upset me. What right did he have to talk to me like that? He was also always on me to move out on my own and get a job. Ummm, I had had a major breakdown. I was sick all the time. Was it really realistic for me to live on my own or hold down a job at that time?

Being a multiple I hear voices in my head. We all have a running self talk we pay little attention to. Well I have selves-talk. I hear the alters talking sometimes. This particular psychiatrist doesn't believe that DID is real. He looked at the voices in my head as being Schizophrenia. When I got to a point I didn't hear any voices, he acted like that was a good thing. Then when the voices started back up again he acted like I had done something wrong, like it was terrible to hear people talking in my head. What was so terrible about it? I mean it wasn't like irrational stuff, urging me to do bad hurtful things, or telling me that a dresser was a tiger or something. That really bothered me a lot. He wasn't even open to the possibility that it wasn't schizophrenic voices. I mean I didn't have any of the other symptoms of Schizophrenia did I?

That is the biggest problem with having DID, the reaction and attitude of medical professionals. I ended up firing another psychiatrist after only one meeting because of the way he treated me. Told me that he was only going to deal with the one who is in charge, who is responsible for making sure I take my medications. He was not going to deal with the DID, but only with the Depression and PTSD. Like the DID didn't even exist as far as he was concerned. He hadn't even read through my file yet, so how would he know.

Then this doctor tricked me into taking an anti-psychotic. It was a low dose but had bad side effects, like shaking and effects on the heart rate. See I already had bouts of shaking so bad I couldn't control my own body. Like an epileptic seizure looks, real violent shaking. That was just from the intensity of the emotional waves running through me, the body releasing its memories. I also have an irregular heartbeat. Plus when I am asleep my heart rate goes way down and sometimes during the day if it went up to around 150 I would get very dizzy and blackout. Not cool when it happens. I didn't need any medication which could mess with my heart. I have enough problems thank you very much.

I know that in the old movies they glamorize fainting. There is nothing glamorous about it. Your sight dims, like someone is slowly putting out the lights. Your legs get very wobbly and you can't stand still. Then boom! There is blackness all around you. The room is spinning like a carnival ride. Your legs fall out from under you and you are down on the ground. I was so lucky I never hit my head on anything when I fell.

When, in the spring of 2003, we all moved to a different house in Berlin, with room for us all, I only needed a few days to get emotionally adjusted. The hardest thing was the windows of this old house reminded me of a farmhouse I used to live in.

That farmhouse, located about a mile or so outside of Elkhorn, was spooky. There was a presence there, a male presence. This presence watched me and I could feel him, even if I couldn't see him. That was real unnerving when you are just a girl and have already been so abused by males, to have this "ghost" watching you in the shower, or looking up at you through your bedroom window. He even projected thoughts and images into my mind, his own fantasies.

What made it worse was that, I was also being molested by a live male and exposed to pornography. I was only about 12 years old at the time. Having two males abusing you like that was a lot for anyone to handle. They took advantage of the changes happening in my body from reaching puberty. They twisted things around to make it my fault and like I wanted all this. They lied to me. I didn't want it. I didn't want it at all and I wished they would leave me alone. I felt sick and scared and dirty and confused. I could hide from the one whenever he came to the house. But how do you hide from a ghost?

I think all these things that had been happening to me from a very young age, maybe even before Lolo (a terrifying thought that makes me shudder inside) was to train me, to make me believe and therefore one day act as if that was my only purpose in being a female, to be used for a man's pleasure. I realize how easy it could have been for them to have succeeded. I very well could have gone to the other extreme, like many girls who have been abused sexually have. You either shut down that part of you completely or become over-sexual. Both responses are unhealthy and a way to hide pain, to hide yourself, but then being abused does not promote health, does it?

There was a long narrow room in the back of the house which I couldn't go into and stayed empty. It was more like a long closet it was so narrow. I felt very uncomfortable every time I ventured in there. Another room in the house was made of cement blocks and was always cold even on the hottest days of summer. I think it was so cold for more reasons than its construction. I hated going in there. Of course, there was a cellar, you accessed from the outside. I couldn't even go anywhere near the door. I am very scared of basements of any kind. For a long time I had a reoccurring nightmare about a bloody lady coming up from a basement. My bedroom window looked out onto the backyard near where this door was. That was the only place I actually saw the ghost. Anywhere else, I only felt him.

I know many people don't believe in that kind of stuff and will think it only an overactive imagination or paranoia from all my years of being abused. But that male "ghost", spirit, whatever was real. I swear, I mean swear, that he followed me after we moved, followed me around for years, even up north here when I moved to Princeton. I wonder too if he was the only spirit being I had encountered. I have a feeling that that there were others before. Something to do with the "bad magic" house, as one of the littles calls a place I lived in near East Troy.

Until I remember I won't really know for sure. If I remember that is. Living under extreme stress and trauma after trauma for an extended span of time makes it harder to record memories as well as retrieve them later. One of the reasons most of my childhood is this huge black blank. It also shuts down the normal growth process, physical, mental, and emotional. Many of the natural steps people go through from infancy to adult, that you are not even aware of going through, I missed. My brain permanently wired for survival in a certain kind of environment. That is one reason why it is so hard to adjust and learn how to cope and engage in a "different" world.

To then be living in a house with similar windows was frightening. When it started to get even a little dark, I flipped on lights. It was hard to sleep. I jumped at every sound. The fear and feeling of similarity with that other house faded away eventually as I settled in and saw all the differences to that other house. Todd helped too. He guided me around by the hand into all the rooms, of the basement in particular, and assured me there were no monsters or ghosts there.

CHAPTER THREE

Many things happened, the year and a half I lived in this house in Berlin. More alters emerged. I now had a total of 11 alters from 6 months old to 20:

Baby or Rosilita (6 months old),
Lolo (3/4),
Rhiannon also known as Nobody (8),
Casey (8),
Fenix (9),
Cindy Ella (10),
Hannah (13/14),
Tia (13),
Cera (16/17),
Red (18),
and Dianah (19/20).

When Baby (or Rosilita) first emerged she would just sit curled up with our blanket, crying, in a lot of pain. She being only 6 months old couldn't talk and would not allow anyone else inside to talk either. My throat was locked up. Though I wanted to talk, and tried to talk, I couldn't, which was very frustrating. Rosilita is easily frightened by loud noises and fighting of any kind. She loves the Spanish language and music. It is one thing that brings her comfort. She likes watching little kid shows and cuddling with her stuffed animals.

Lolo by being out and playing with Claire and studying her math (Algebra of all things) aged to four years old. She is very smart and loves learning things. Being very social and friendly she helps new insiders as they emerge, taking them by the hand and showing them around our inner safe place. She loves animals and movies and books.

Rhiannon when she came out said her name was Nobody. That is how she felt about herself. She had little to no self-esteem, everything was her fault. She was good for nothing, not fit for anything. All the negative images of myself I had, she carried as well as the negative images others told me I was, like stupid and lazy, and ugly. Through therapy, both inner with me and outer with Lynn and Louise*, she came to realize that she was somebody. Not everything was her fault. She does have talents and interests that are important and have been important to the survival of me. I was reading a book about the young Merlin and he had a sister named Rhiannon, Rhia for short, who lived in a tree and loved nature. Nobody liked nature too. It was the only place she found any peace. It seemed a most fitting name for her.

Casey was the tape recorder. All the negative, nasty, audible abuses she would be forced to play back, to continue the abuse and keep me down. One night while doing this, each word, put into a masculine voice for greater effect, was like a physical blow to me. I felt like I was being beat up by an invisible demon. I heard crying inside my head and a little girl's voice saying that she didn't want to do this anymore, but she couldn't find the off button. The bigger insiders gathered around her and helped her to smash the tape recorder, freeing her. Her name came from a movie, where a kid named Casey was picked on and beat up on a regular basis, but in the end becomes a hero. She is much happier being free and loves to play computer and video games and isn't afraid of a little healthy competition.

Fenix and Casey are inseparable. At first after Casey was freed, I would hear them competing against each other at some game on the computer, trying to outdo each other's scores. They would laugh and tease, calling each other names in a friendly way. Together they are my little warrior and are very brave and a strength to me when things get hard or I am under attack from the outside world. Casey has indeed become a hero.

Cindy Ella is as her name suggests. She is the one who keeps things neat and clean and organized. She used to be quite particular about things and would get very upset if the wrong utensil was used. She was so afraid that if things weren't just so that she would get into "trouble", which usually meant a beating. She loves to cook. Even though she is well organized and so particular, when it comes to cooking, recipes are mere suggestions to her. She loves to be creative and experiment with spices and different combinations. Sometimes they work out great, sometimes they don't. She isn't afraid anymore about getting into trouble if things are just so and has relaxed a lot. She still hates being dirty, but she no longer freaks out if one of the littles wants to splash in puddles, or play in the sand or leaves.

Hannah is a typical teenager. She is outgoing and funny and flirty. She used to wear braids in her hair as a sure sign that it was her who was out. In fact, I am trying to grow my hair out again so she can wear her braids again. She loves music and dancing and movies that are funny or full of action or scary. She likes to read young adult books about fellow teenagers. There was a doll that came out at one time named Hannah Rose. She was a redhead with braids and held a slate in her hands which she had written, "I will not hit boys. I will not hit boys. I will hit boys and I am not sorry." That is just like my Hannah, her playfulness.

Tia, me, I keep things together. I help build communication lines between alters and maintain a common memory bank so that all know what each other is basically doing, so there are less blackouts and time losses and confusion. I study constantly about a variety of things and by doing so have been able to do a lot of inner therapy work. I call inner conferences when there is a big issue to deal with, like doctor appointments. I hold back judgments and conclusions about a matter until I have more facts or information to see a bigger, clearer picture. I know some of the other insiders get mad at me, because I try to help them see behind a person's actions to what may be really going on. Sometimes they just want to be mad or to hate that person. I assure them, understanding another person's problems doesn't mean it was okay to be treated badly and they don't have to be friends with them if they don't want to.

I am a back-seater. What this means is that I sit in the back seat while other insiders go about the business of living life. I am afraid to live. Funny, how I can help all the others inside and out and can't help myself. In a way my faith was a way to hide from life, from trying. Living like a nun, I could concentrate on everyone else and put myself last. I never really did get to me though did I? I sometimes try holding the other insiders back, keeping them from aging, from healing too quickly. I am afraid of loosing my usefulness. See I know a little bit about a lot of different things and hate looking stupid, sometimes stating the obvious and coming off as a know-it-all, when really I don't know a lot about any one thing. It is all a hodge-podge. My pool of knowledge is growing as I study more and observe others, but I still feel lost when it comes to who I am. I don't know and I am scared to find out. I stopped aging, stopped living at 13, because life was just too hard. I don't know how to get started again and am still very afraid.

Cera is now 17 and vivacious. She is social and friendly and a wonderful girl. Though she still struggles with her self-image and how others see her.

Red sometimes talks with a southern accent, a more romantic type image maybe. The parts of me she carries, my sexuality, romanticism, sensuality, my heart, are bit by bit coming to life. I am not sure how to handle all these new feelings especially with such a traumatic past. I am not sure that I will ever be able to utilize all that I am as a female, because of those traumas, maybe in time with healing.

Dianah is my warrior princess. When she first emerged she said of herself that she was like Zena without the leather. I think she may be rethinking that leather issue though. The first thing she did when she revealed herself is write Jake a note asking him to stop treating Cera as he was. Dianah was aware of how Jake was using Cera's emotions towards him to keep her hanging on yet also keep her at a distance and all confused. Dianah said she would "kick his ass" if he didn't stop hurting Cera. Of course, Jake is like 20 times stronger if not more than Dianah and had more fighting skills than her, so it was more the force of words than a real threat. But it did scare Jake. Esther has an alter who did get violent and was very strong and maybe he feared Dianah was similar. All that came of that fear though was he blocked his door and went and stayed at Todd's for a week. His behavior never changed. So maybe he wasn't afraid of Dianah at all but just used her as an excuse to run away.

***

It was here, in Berlin, I discovered the truth of my parentage. How totally flooring that was! The woman I had believed was my mother. The name I had lived under for so long. A lot of my personal history. All had been lies or partial truths.

It started with a memory of a woman with long softly curled auburn hair. I was on her lap and she was singing to me as she rocked and gently rubbed my hands, which were hurting from arthritis. I was only an infant, small and in a lot of pain. She called me her little Rose. I knew, just knew that this woman was my mother, my real mother. That this also was the woman in the first flashback I had had. That was why I had felt an affection for her. She was my birth mother.

When I told Jake and his family about it, they didn't believe me. They thought it was just a dream. I had made her up because I didn't want to deal with the truth about my past and what my parents had done to me. They treated Rose as just another alter and refused to believe that it was me, who I was meant to be when I was born. They refused to believe my true age too. They refused to believe many things. Like all they would accept was what they wanted to believe, what they could handle, what they needed and wanted me to be and nothing else. All the rest, well, wasn't real.

My therapist believed me though. I actually had two therapists for a while. Lynn came over to the house and was helping me to get out and about, even if just to the library once a week and was helping me with my socializing. The other, named Louise, was for the traumas and heavy issues. I traveled two hours one way to see her, twice a month. She was worth it, though.

I think the whole point of Jake's parents getting me to see this second therapist, Louise, was that they didn't like Lynn. Coming to the house like she did she saw things, like how I was being treated, how isolated I was being kept. She kept trying to get me to move out of the house. But I was too scared to start over. I felt about Jake and his family like they were my family, even if I wasn't always treated like I should be.

I think too, because Louise was a no nonsense kind of woman, they hoped that she would prove I was "faking" everything and I would then be forced to become what they wanted me to be. It didn't work out that way. Instead, Louise proved I was telling the truth. She also knew how I was being treated and agreed with Lynn that I needed to get out of there and to stand up for myself more instead of being a doormat.

See the truth is, that I was being abused and taken advantage of and treated more like a servant than a person, by Jake's family and, well, sometimes even by him. Not the obvious abuses that you think of when you hear the word. It was those subtler kinds.

I know I am not an easy person to live with and I go through many things that are real difficult to handle, especially when my world started falling apart. I know that I am far from perfect. I also like cooking and don't mind cleaning and taking care of kids, all that. I don't mind helping out, doing my share. There were things I liked doing, like the dishes, other people in the house hated doing. Besides, doing the dishes was good for my achy hands. The point is the attitude I got. If I didn't do it because I was working through something and needed time to myself, or because I wasn't feeling well, I was called all kinds of terrible names and they would bitch and moan. If I did it, there was complaining that "I didn't cook it like mom does" or that "I was taking over". I couldn't win.

All my money that came in went to household expenses, every cent. *(I had applied for SSI (Supplemental Security Income) and started receiving a check every month soon after we moved to Berlin. I had little choice. I couldn't work and needed the health insurance for my treatment.)* Four adults in that house with income coming in, five when Jake's sister, Vicki, and her kids moved back in with us, but I paid half the rent and utilities and all of the phone bill since it was in my name, though I rarely made any phone calls. Esther paid the other half of the rent, utilities, and the renter's insurance, which we needed to have because of her animals.

Esther and I had a joint checking account. I had thought it would be easier to pay the bills that way, with both our money being automatically deposited on the 1st and

3rd of the month. In the beginning of the month, I would sit at the table and write out the checks for the bills. To keep the checkbook straight, I needed to know about all automatic payments, checks written, and debit card uses, so I could be sure there was enough money to cover the basic bills. I would get upset if checks were written on a hope and a prayer that the money would be deposited on time or if they would do heavy shopping on the last day of the month knowing my check would be deposited on the first to cover it. One month I had to cover $200 worth of overdraft and bounced check fees. That was no picnic.

When I stressed the importance of waiting to go shopping till the main bills were paid and to let me know what was spent, well that didn't go over well. Esther accused me of being too controlling and that she had to have my permission to spend any money. What was I to do after we kept receiving overdraft notices or weren't able to write out a check for groceries because of a bounced check? It was okay if I didn't have any money for even the basics, or just a little even for myself. I had trouble even coming up with the $1 co-pay for the chiropractor I had started to see for my chronic back pain. *(Turns out I had some discs that were very deteriorated in my lower back, which were also arthritic, a curve in my spine, whiplash in my neck, and arthritis in my hips.)* But it wasn't okay for me to know what money was going out to ensure that it could be covered, that bills could be paid. Does that sound right to you? It didn't to me either.

Jake did help out during the summers when he was able to work two jobs. Since he was still in school, he could only work part time most of the year. I greatly appreciated his doing that. It helped relieve some of the financial burden on Esther and me for those months. James also worked, but where all his money went even he didn't know. He wasn't very good at managing money.

For the most part, we were all living off of what Esther and I brought in. I am used to being poor and struggling financially. The problem wasn't that all my money went for bills. The problem, and the abuse, was that it was okay that I was paying more than my share of things on top of everything else I took care of around the house. It was all in the attitude and their responses to things, how they talked to me and tried to make me feel. I felt like I was paying them to be their housekeeper. It was usually my fault when there wasn't enough money for this or that. I was being too nosey when an overdraft notice came in and I had to figure out why and asked them what they had spent and how much. What? I was to make funds appear out of nowhere? Wave my magic wand so that they could do what they wanted to?

One thing that Lynn witnessed and both therapists were aware of, was the behavior of James. He was a big man with a big voice who liked using it to intimidate. He had learned it from his father. He knew how it frightened both me and his wife, how it controlled his own son's behavior and attitude. He did not care. He liked that power and used it. He would not change it, no matter what. He could be a nice caring man. No person is completely bad, right? However, he liked too much me being afraid of him. Yet at the same time would make me feel bad for being afraid of him. He said he would never hit anyone, but his words and tone were as much a hit as if he had used his hand.

James grew to hate my relationship with Jake, that closeness that still existed in a way between him and Cera. He often made me feel stupid and small, as though I didn't know anything. I was just to take care of the house and stuff and not have any kind of life of my own. Nothing was good enough. To him I was too "old" to even be friends with Jake. Yet when I started talking with a man in New York who was 31, he was "too old" for me. See, I couldn't win. I think a lot of it was from his wanting me to be his little sister. She had died very young and I guess I reminded him of her and resembled her in a way. I couldn't take her place and did not want to, which frustrated him.

For the most part, I got along well with Esther, for the most part. Her littles got along with mine and enjoyed things together, like reading and games. When one particular little, who easily was frightened, was having a rough spell, she would respond to me. Many times, when I was experiencing something, I could talk to one of her bigs. She understood so much having gone through it herself. I looked at her as a kind of mother figure and even called her "Mom", out of respect to her.

Esther had other alters who seemed to not like me much and would sometimes lash out in one way or another. Like the accusation that I was faking. Or calling me some name because of Cera's friendship with Jake. Or saying that I was taking over things, because I was doing so much in the house that used to be her job. See, she ended up in a wheel chair for three years, from the intensity of her migraines, and could no longer do all the housework and things that she used to take care of. Though no longer needing the wheelchair, she couldn't physically handle all the housework. That is why I had moved in with them to begin with. She did as much as she could when she could of course, but it is easy to fall behind and get overwhelmed. I think she resented having to have help. I understand that feeling. But still, it wasn't right to take it out on me.

Esther also thought that I was keeping her grandkids from her sometimes. Fear and depression really warps one's view of things. I know it has mine. It was hard to know when it was okay to let them go into her room when she was stuck in bed and when not to. Since I would be yelled at no matter what I did in that regard, I just did the best I could. As well as with the daily care of these two little ones of Vicky's. To have me doing a lot of the caretaking left Jake's parents free for other things, yet they resented me. Nice sticky situation, huh?

With certain of Esther's alters, I think there was jealousy going on there behind some of her behavior towards me. Now, I am not this vain girl, thinking I am all that. I know that I am not, far from it. I struggle with my self-image as much as most people do, probably more. Anyone who has been abused to the degree I have can't think too much of themselves. It was more like I didn't think enough of myself, didn't place enough value on me as a person. When I say that people were jealous it isn't out of vanity, but observation of behavior. I kind of can do that, distance myself and see a bigger picture. Drives some of the others inside nuts and yet the truths it uncovers are helpful to all of them and other people.

I was blooming, reaching out and free to try to experience life. While Esther felt trapped. Some of her alters being young, felt imprisoned within the body of a mother and grandmother, hampered by all those responsibilities from being free to be themselves as they would have liked to, as they saw me doing.

Vicky, Jake's sister, is a nice woman with her own set of problems, things from her own traumatic past. With her it was more of a taking me and all I did for granted and taking advantage of my quietness and inability to say no. She also didn't understand the things I was going through, the way I felt and reacted to certain things and would tease or give me a hard time. She gave me a hard time too in regards to the friendship with Jake. More from her own feelings about her half brother, I believe, than it had to do with me. *(That seems to be how it is with many people and how they treat others, I have found. Something inside them, some pain or disappointment, or lack in their own life that they project outwards. I told you I was the therapist, didn't I?)*

All the things that happened and how his family reacted to me changed how Jake treated me. It was a confusing mix. Sometimes he was a friend. We would hang out, talk, play a computer game, listen to music, watch a movie or TV show. Other times I didn't even exist. He would treat me like a piece of furniture when he brought friends over. Then he would claim that it was because I would get all upset when he brought someone over. Wouldn't you get upset if hardly anyone outside the house even knew you existed much less lived in the house and couldn't be introduced, though everyone else was? He could tell them I was an adopted sister, couldn't he? In a way, it was the truth.

Although I was reaching out best I could to socialize, the internet really being my only outlet, Jake would do things to keep me hanging on by a thread. Now being friends is okay and acting as such. But it was like he wanted my attention on him and not on some other guy, especially when he was between girlfriends. I was someone to fall back on. Who he knew would always be there. Being isolated as I was pretty much guaranteed there wasn't any competition, not any real competition. Content as I was to love him just as a friend, these other behaviors would keep those romantic dreams alive or focused on him.

For instance after getting home from the hospital Jake would get real mad when he saw Todd sitting on the swing in the yard next to me. We were just talking, laughing, but he was furious. Mad at me or Todd I don't know. What? Todd was supposed to ignore me or something? I wasn't allowed to talk to any other male without things being assumed? Please.

Then there was an incident when Jake was working on the roof of the house we lived in. Our landlord ran a construction company and Jake started working for him. Good money and he liked the work. He looked very masculine and kind of sexy all dirty after a hard day, which helped drive part of me crazy. Anyways, another guy, good looking too, working for the company, was helping him with the roof. One day they were taking their lunch break. I was outside with Jake's niece and nephew. The guy came over to the patio and sat across from me. We were just having a normal, generic conversation, no big deal. Jake went to go sit next to me on the swing, then changed his mind and sat on a chair instead. I felt like he was telling this guy don't even think about it in case you were. Hand's off.

There were the times he would watch me sunbathing in my swimsuit from an upstairs window. Not to mention he would find excuses to walk into the bathroom we shared while I was in the shower. Or the many looks across the room with his eyes all warm and dark. Maybe it was just a normal male response to a blooming female. Point is it kept me holding onto hope and directed my awakening as a woman towards him. Then he would deny any of it and tell me I was hallucinating. Oh really? I have an imagination, but not that good a one. Talk about confusing. Not to mention using my emotional and mental condition as a "get out of jail free" card. If he had no feelings for me, wasn't "attracted" in any way, then why not leave me alone? Why play these games with my mind and heart?

My therapists kept trying to get me to go out more, meet other people, form relationships with other males. If I couldn't make sense of Jake's behavior, couldn't trust the signals I seemed to get at times from him, then how could I from any other male? How would I know if a guy was just flirting or if he really liked me? I have no experience for that kind of thing. Even those with experience are confused and unsure aren't they? I would have been completely lost and constantly hurt. Could I really risk all that?

One of the biggest problems I had with Jake was his addiction to pornography. Now of course being heavily sexually abused as I was, that aspect of being human, sexuality, was a very scary issue. To me it was all about pain, being used, treated as an object, and tossed aside to be forgotten. That was why I was and still am to a degree afraid of men and had avoided sex completely. That someone I trusted, considered a friend, felt safe with, was engaging in that kind of behavior was very difficult, especially for the littles.

The view that pornography was normal behavior between two people made it worse. Not just because pornography was used in my abuse, perhaps to a greater extent than I am even currently aware of, but that it dehumanizes females. It makes them just body parts. Sexuality becomes just one person's gratification, cold, empty, even cruel.

It is a very addictive thing. The internet makes it so easy. I know that Red, in dealing with our sexuality explored it a bit herself. She found it drawing her, stimulating something in her mind, and at first something in her body, but that soon wore off. It wasn't enough, the images. Not to mention so much of it was obviously staged and unrealistic. A maximization of exposure of sexual body parts more than anything and more geared towards men or towards same sex sexuality. Yet it was hard for her to get away from and the images would stick in her mind. What finally broke it, before it became a real problem, was it was triggering one of the littles. There are sites dealing with pornographic pictures of young girls, preteens and early teens. Something about it really upset her, like she had been forced to have such pictures taken of her. That is the feeling I got. As a child, we certainly were used by men. Just the portrayal of young girls acting like they want to be used like that was, well terrible. This alter would not revel her memories concerning it though or even which one she was. She still hasn't.

Several of the insiders, including me, were concerned about the effect Jake's viewing such things so much would have on him. Mixed with the influence of those guy magazines, not the pornographic ones most are familiar with, but ones that are just as bad. In the articles were such lies like, that it is okay to force a woman to have sex, saying "no" was just a game women play. Most women like to have sex in public places, being viewed by others having sex. Virgins were the worst to have intercourse with, but gave the best "head". It is okay to play "mind games". On and on.

Jake valued this misinformation. He didn't see anything wrong with viewing women as just body parts, or viewing me as just body parts and not always as a person. He built up the sexual tension between us the spring and summer of 2004, until it burst over the edges. Even with his minimal experience, he knew just how to play me. I was lost, just too inexperienced and ignorant, too hungry for love. It made it too easy for him to play with my emotions.

CHAPTER FOUR

I feel a little torn right now. As if, I am being ungracious to Jake and his family and am giving the impression that they were "bad" people. I appreciate all that they did for me. They took me back into their home after I had that complete breakdown instead of tossing me out on the street. They may have said I was like family, but I really wasn't. They were under no obligations to me.

Sure, in many ways they felt like family. I grew to care about all of them in some way, even if it wasn't how they wanted it to be. There were a lot of good times and like I said, I wasn't easy to live with because of all I was going through. As far as I was concerned they were family, and you take the good with the bad, right?

But then again, being a family, caring about someone, even if not blood related, is no excuse for abuse or to be silent about it. I was silent for way too long. One of the biggest factors in developing DID is everything is a secret, you can't talk to anyone about what is happening, not even yourself. So although it may make me look disloyal, or unappreciative, I must speak the truth of what happened to me, of how I felt, how it added to the already warped view I had of myself from my past.

Being not believed. Being forced to be something I wasn't. Having what I was feeling dismissed. Understanding when Jake's mom was going through something and needed time, but not me. Teasing me, belittling me, making me feel bad because all these things were happening to me. All these added to my feelings of being worthless, not valued, not loveable, cursed. It wasn't just from the depression and low self-esteem. It was from how I was being treated, viewed as a person by those around me. If I did what they wanted, acted how they wanted, was just a silent machine, that was fine. If I didn't or couldn't, it wasn't. I had to be patient and understanding, aware of and deal with their moods, pet peeves, illnesses and all, but I was not being extended the same curtsey.

***

I was in a strange, confusing, and frightening place with my healing. To have these feelings and needs awaken in me yet still be terrified of sex, terrified of the male sex organ itself. That is understandable when you have been so severely abused at a young age, when that part was used like a weapon to hurt you. Part of me thrilled at how Jake looked at me and how it made me feel at times so beautiful and alive and warm, but it also scared me.

Not all of my sexual abuse was physical, some was mental with the pornography. Some was just by how I was looked at. When some men looked at me they didn't see a girl at all, my youth, my innocence. They only saw a female. I was violated with their eyes even if they never laid a hand on me. I was stripped down in their mind to only one thing. Although I now had these womanly natural feelings, I was still that little abused girl too. Even today, I can not stand being looked at that way. I still feel violated, demeaned as a person and as a female.

There was an incident that happened with Todd that illustrates this I think. He was staying the weekend the spring of 2003, shortly after we had moved in. I was working on digging a garden and he and Jake were helping turn the dirt over and taking out the huge stones. His behavior towards me was a little different from the usual light flirting we sometimes did.

He tossed these little stones at me, always missing me but coming close. Jake was right there and told him to stop in a quiet voice, nothing more. He commented on how I looked. He gently ran a finger down my cheek. I didn't know what to make of it. He was aware of my feelings towards Jake, and my belief that I would never feel like that with anyone else, because of how hurt I had been and my inability to reach out in trust. He couldn't understand though why I held onto those feelings when Jake wasn't interested in me.

Looking back, the reason I held onto those feelings for Jake was mostly a fear that I wouldn't find myself attracted to anyone else combined with a need to be normal. I was afraid to think, to believe a girl like me could be really liked by some guy, so I clung hard to a fantasy. In my innocence and inexperience, I made more of those friend-like feelings of caring and enjoying his company than I should have. And like I said, I hadn't been loved or cared about in a long, long time. Jake was the first one to see me and reach out to me as a person. I wasn't sure, how could I believe, that it wasn't just a fluke?

Though, I liked Todd some, thought of him as a friend, I was too afraid and unsure of myself. I didn't know how to interpret his actions. I was ignorant on how I am supposed to respond or not respond and afraid to make a mistake.

Then one evening while Jake was out for a run, Todd walked me upstairs to my room. It was late and I was tired from all that work in the garden. He put on some quiet music and tucked me in. That was sweet wasn't it? He asked if he could rub my back to help me go to sleep. I said no. I did not tell him I was very uncomfortable with being touched. That it had unnerved me some when he had touched my cheek. That I felt Jake was so unique compared to the rest of males, since his touch and presence had been comforting not scary, safe. At least it had been back at the beginning.

Todd began to rub my stomach. Just gentle circular motions over the blankets, but my back started to hurt and I began to panic. I told him that my back was hurting and for him to stop. He didn't understand. He said it was supposed to feel good not hurt. Well, for a normal girl it would, but I am not a normal girl. When he didn't stop I got even more scared. I think I had to tell him like three times and by then the panic was obvious in my face, so he stopped. He told me before he left that there are other guys out there. Did he mean him or just in general? Is that what all this was about?

I was now scared of him. I had said to stop and he didn't. Red flags came up. I didn't know what to think or how to react. I talked with Lynn about it. I had to be careful how much I told her though. She made sure I understood that she is also a court advocate and that she would have to report it if he hadn't stopped and more had happened. Being he was only 17 at the time, I would be more than likely the one to get into trouble, even if I hadn't done anything wrong. Though there was a case going through the courts at the time concerning a woman who was a multiple. Still, that scared me just as much as what happened or what I feared could have happened rather.

A few months passed and Todd and his brother were going to stay with us because their parents were going to be out of town. I was worried about that. I had told Jake's parents that Todd had scared me and they looked out for me whenever Todd came over after that, not leaving me alone in the house or even in a room with him. Todd didn't understand why I was scared of him, what he had done. While he was there with his brother, I decided to talk to him about it. I felt ready to talk to him about it.

We went for a walk, my suggestion so that we wouldn't be overheard, but downtown where there was also people about and traffic. I was honest with him about how I reacted to what he had done. "It scared me when I had told you to stop and you didn't."

He said, "I hadn't heard you say stop or I would have. I was just trying to help you relax and go to sleep. I did not mean to hurt or scare you." He told me he did like me, that we were friends, and he wanted me to know that there are other guys out there who would like me, instead of holding out for someone who doesn't seem to.

I am glad I talked to him and was honest. It is better to pay attention to my red flags, even if I misinterpret them, than to ignore them. The flags are there for a reason. It was a positive step to take to talk with him, to confront him, and deal with my reactions, than to just stay in fear of him.

I noticed that in the on-line chat rooms light flirting was okay. I could flirt back and had a lot of good, clean fun. If it started to get too heavy, however, I would start to feel sick to my stomach and scared. At the one sight I usually went to, the men were more mature and respectful. They did not tease me or call me names when I told them it was too much. They could tell by how I talked that I was young and inexperienced and they backed off. That helped so much in my healing. Not all men are disrespectful or see women as objects to use.

The spring of 2004, Memorial Weekend in fact, a whole year after that incident with Todd, I received my first kiss. Todd was staying over. He needed to get away from home and was thinking of moving in with all of us. That would have been cool, since we had become good friends. We had been sending e-mails back and forth, talking about all kinds of different things. We were able to talk about things that we couldn't with other people. It would be nice to be able to hang with someone who accepted me as I was, even if he didn't understand it all. At least he tried to.

One day we were having a great time sitting upstairs talking, playing chess, listening to music, flirting a little bit. We started to dance. He leaned in and kissed me. It was a light little peck on the lips. I didn't feel what I expected to, just cold and empty. No warmth, no spark, not for either one of us. We were just friends after all. There was nothing more than that.

I had wanted to feel, to experience more than the pain I had known, to be able to balance it all out somehow. There was such a need in me to be held, touched in a good, positive, tender way, to be loved. Too great a need. Todd helped in a way. I don't think I was yet quite ready, or he just wasn't the right one to experience more than friendship type affection with.

No, he wasn't the right person. More happened that afternoon than just a simple kiss. More that Todd wanted and I felt pushed into. I felt manipulated afterwards. He kept saying I was the one in control. But those were just empty words. Todd was in control and knew it. He could have pushed for more, wanted to. It was only that it was "my time of month" that prevented it. I kept switching. Sometimes little and so scared and just being submissive, letting him do whatever to get it over with. Fighting would only make me get hurt. Lessons learned very well a long time ago. A big, unsure and scared, just wanting to try, to be, to feel like a normal girl, for him to like her.

Maybe I made the mistake talking to him about all my pain and wanting, needing to feel something else. Made a mistake in trusting him and that friendship. After all he was a guy and had made other "moves" before with me. Here I was so desperate to feel something, anything good. I had all these awakening feelings in me that I did not know how to handle. He read me very well. He said that it would be a kind of therapy for me. His way to justify what he wanted from me, and to keep it from being anything more, from meaning anything. He kept pushing it. I felt scared and uncomfortable, yet I was so…in so much pain.

You have to understand. I was having all these nightmares and flashbacks, body memories of being raped and abused. It had been going on for weeks, months. I was so lost, so depressed, in deep despair. Jake hadn't even hugged me since I came home from the hospital. A few times Esther held me, or hugged me. The only other contact, physical contact I had with another human being was Claire and Alex, holding them, dancing with them, playing with them. But it wasn't enough to fight all that was going on in me. I needed to be held, to be touched in a safe way by a big person, not just a child. The children in me had been abused by adults after all. There were bigs who wanted to live, to experience, to be normal and were feeling all these feelings.

I wanted to be held. I wanted to be loved. I didn't want to have sex with Todd. There wasn't that chemistry, that desire like there was with Jake. Todd was just a friend, that was all. A great guy, good looking, smart, fun, but it just wasn't there between us, least not for me. So why did he want me, at least act like he did and not for the first time? Why did I not push him away and change the subject when it was making me uncomfortable? Did I want to get back at Jake too? Why even bring up that need within me and the things I was contemplating? How stupid to tell him about talking to some guy on-line who was only interested in sex from me and actually thinking about it. Showing him the few pictures I had kept in a drawer of lovers in embrace, which he asked to see.

I didn't want cold, empty sex. I wanted tenderness and love and passion. That would be the only thing to balance, to begin to balance all the violence locked in my body. I didn't believe, I really didn't believe, that I would ever be loved, could be loved like that. I didn't think that I could feel any real pleasure after so much pain for so long.

Yeah, Todd wasn't the right person, wasn't the one I wanted. But he was willing and kept pushing me, and I was in a compromised emotional state. I couldn't think clearly. I was caught between fear and this intense need for human contact, for warmth, for tenderness. And Todd was gentle with what he did and guided me to do. In that way he helped. He took advantage, knew what to do, how to push me. But it cured me from wanting some empty encounter with a stranger. That wasn't what I needed, wanted.

I was glad, relived in a way that Todd had to go back home. I hated that he had to go back to an abusive home, but I knew he wanted to continue using me in that way. I was isolated and no one would have to know. Living there he would have free access to me. He knew it. Knew he could get away with it too, cause who would believe me? Who would really care? It would be too easy to blame me for everything if we were caught, after all who saw me as I really was? To all of them I was a grown woman, not a child, not a young adult. They didn't even believe I was inexperienced, but thought I was lying or just didn't remember. I wasn't strong enough to stand up against it. I was just too confused, too needy, and too vulnerable.

Summer came and the tension between Jake and I increased. He kept looking at me, watching me. I was exercising nearly every night and all that hard work was paying off. I was taking good care of myself, wearing makeup, doing my hair, taking more care with my clothes, how I wore them. I felt prettier and more alive. I was starting to stand up for myself more too. I took one day off a week from cooking. I was able to say no, if I didn't want to do something. I was seriously thinking of moving out on my own and starting to get prepared for that. I think Jake was responding to all that. Responding to the healthier, more alive person I was, compared to the broken mess from before. He also was aware that guys were starting to show some interest in me, even if only a superficial interest.

The middle of July, during those hot, sultry days and nights, the tension burst the banks and flooded over. I had been getting up at 4:15 in the morning to watch Jake's niece and nephew. They were dropped off at 5 a.m., since Vicki worked first shift. I had gotten up as usual. The bathroom was off a large bedroom at the end of the hall. Mostly this room was used for exercising and when Jake's niece and nephew or Todd stayed overnight. In it was a large mattress, a portable clothes rack Jake used to hang some of his clothes on, and my CD player with some CDs. Jake and I shared the bathroom. His parents had their own bathroom on the first floor off their bedroom.

Jake surprised me when I came out of the bathroom and he was standing there. He usually was still asleep this early and he hadn't made any noise. I figured that he would just go back to bed after using the bathroom and thought no more of it. After I finished dressing and was halfway down the dark stairs, Jake called my name. I stopped. He spoke my name again. There was a tone in his voice, and I thought that something was wrong. I climbed back up the stairs and walked down the hallway to where he stood in the gloom between our two bedroom doors.

When I got near Jake wrapped his arms around me and pulled me closer. I put my arms around his shoulders and asked him if he was okay, if he had a bad dream, which he has had from time to time, just as I sometimes did. Jake responded that he was okay and he held me tighter. Then he turned his head and kissed me.

Oh my. My breathe caught. This is what I imagined a kiss would be like. My heart raced. My body melted into his. I dropped the book I was holding in my hand and just clung to him as my knees weakened. His kiss deepened and I was swept away.

He turned around and started to walk me down the hallway to my bedroom. I was lost in a haze of emotions and all the sensations running through my body. He didn't speak as he laid me down on my bed, undid my shorts, and gently pulled them off my hips and down my legs. I reminded him that I had never done this before as he removed my panties. He just shook his head up and down, acknowledging what I had said. I removed the rest of my clothes as he slipped out of his pajama bottoms and slid a condom on.

Jake came over me and tried, but my body would not let him enter. He moved next to me and we kissed some more and began to touch each other. It felt so good. I wasn't afraid in any way. Not of him or his body. Not of what was happening. Not of how he was touching the most sensitive parts of me that had been so violated when I was so young. Finally, a healing. Finally, a normality.

Jake jumped when he heard a car door slam shut and quickly got off my bed, grabbed his pajamas, and left the room, thinking it was his sister. I got up and glanced out of the window as I dressed. It wasn't his sister, must have been the neighbor, but she would be there soon anyways.

As I was ready to go downstairs to wait for Vicky and the kids, Jake came into my room again. He had a big smile on his face. He asked me not to tell anyone about this, what had happened. I told him I wasn't planning to, that it was between me and him. We hugged and kissed again. Then I went downstairs and he went back to his room.

Vicky's children were little, her daughter Claire* was 3, her son, Alex* almost 2. They rarely went back to sleep after they arrived so I was on the go from 5 am until Vicky came to pick them up in the afternoon or early evening, or if they spent the night until they finally went to sleep. My only break was if I was able to get them down for a nap.

I was flying high all that morning. I played with the kids: singing, dancing, tickle wrestling. I didn't know what this all meant, what would happen. I really thought I was content just being friends with Jake. I never really believed that anything like this would happen, that I would feel so good, so free, so unafraid. I figured he would be cool when he came downstairs, not say or do anything other than was normal in case his parents were around. But when he came down, he didn't say anything, not one word. He didn't even look at me. He just walked into the living room, sat down on the couch, and turned on the TV.

His parents were not home. We were there alone with Vicky's two children, who were playing good on the front porch where all their toys were kept. I got anxious as time went by and he still didn't do or say anything. I finally asked him if he remembered if anything had happened that morning. *(He has slept-walked in the past and not remembered what he had said or done. It was possible he thought it had been a dream and not real, or that he didn't remember at all. God forbid.)* He didn't respond at first. I asked him again. Then he said he didn't remember anything happening. I had known it was a possibility, to hear him say it though, that he didn't remember, when it was so clear and vivid in my mind and my body, well that hit hard and I didn't know what to do.

Sally, Jake's friend from Beloit, had been calling and talking to me every day, several times a day. She had broken up with her boyfriend and needed someone to talk to someone to listen. She called right after Jake told me he didn't remember. As I talked to her, I started to cry. She asked what was wrong and I refused to tell her. I couldn't tell her, couldn't tell anyone, but I needed to talk to someone, to a girlfriend. She might know what to do. I told Jake to watch the kids a minute while I went outside with the phone. I told Sally what had happened. I poured it out to her, the basics and how I felt. She listened and didn't call me names or freak out. She was very understanding. She told me to talk to him, tell him what happened. It was good advice.

I went back into the house and told the kids to stay on the porch and play. I told Jake we needed to talk. I again asked him if he remembered anything happening that morning. He still denied it, but there was something in his eyes, a sparkle. I had a feeling that he wasn't telling the truth. Sometimes, especially when you have known someone a long time, you can tell when they are lying. I started telling him pieces, starting from when he surprised me when I came out of the bathroom. That he called my name when I had been going downstairs. That he took me into his arms and kissed me. That more happened in my bedroom.

He said, "I hope I didn't do something stupid, like having sex with you." The way he said it and the look in his eyes, I knew for sure then that he did indeed remember. I think he lied because he was afraid of my reaction to it. Maybe he thought that I would freak and be afraid of him. I don't blame him considering my reactions in the past to finding his pornography and when Vicky's boyfriend would sit out in the living room watching that stuff. How scared and upset it had made me. Not to mention how I reacted last year to Todd's just rubbing my stomach.

Jake's parents came home so we couldn't talk any further about it. Lynn arrived to take me out to the library. I ran up to my room to get my purse. Jake was upstairs and I asked him if we could talk later after he came home from work. He worked two jobs. It was his second job that he was getting ready for, the one he had all year round.

He said we could and asked me. "Did you tell Sally about what had happened?"

I lied to him and said I hadn't. Well, what was I supposed to say? What would you say? Exactly. And well I was planning on telling him the truth later when we talked. Neither of us had the time right then to get into it. Besides,

I think he already knew that I had, that that was why I took the phone outside.

Jake said, "I'm sorry." I didn't know what he was sorry about, if it was for lying to me about not remembering or that he had kissed me and we had ended up having sex.

As I walked down the stairs I said, "I'm not." Well, I wasn't. Not then anyways. Maybe I should have been. After all, I had given in to him way to easily. Did that make me a "bad girl", just going along with him, not thinking, just feeling?

It was a Thursday morning when this happened between us. We didn't get a chance to talk that night when he got home from work. Vicky's children were staying overnight since Alex was going to be going to visit his dad for two weeks. They wouldn't go to sleep and Jake's parents had gone to bed. Convenient, huh. That weekend he was busy. If it wasn't work then it was something he had to do with his friends. The little he was home we were never alone.

One cute thing occurred with Jake's niece, Claire on that Saturday. She is jealous when it comes to me. She doesn't like to share me with anyone, not even her brother. I was her Auntie Rose. She liked it when I was little because we had a lot of fun together playing. I have one little, Lolo, around the same age as her and they had a blast together. Claire had a friend and that made up a little bit for her not having a daddy that she was able to go visit like Alex, her brother, did.

Well, this day, I was sitting on one end of the couch and Jake was sitting at the other end. Claire came over and told Jake to sit by me. When he didn't move, she told him it was okay he could sit by me. This was her way of saying she approved of him and me, that she was willing to share me with him. That's a pretty big sacrifice for a 3 year old. When he said no and stayed at the other end of the couch, a look came over her face, part disappointment, and part that she thought her uncle was being silly. She climbed up and sat between us and both Jake and I ended up tickling her. Jake's dad was sitting across the room, watching as we laughed. It gave me a strange feeling. Just something about the way he was watching us.

Monday came. Jake came home from working construction all sunburned on his back. He took his shirt off in front of me so his mother could rub lotion on it. Usually he was embarrassed and uncomfortable to do that in front of me and would go into his parent's bedroom. He had a sparkle in his eyes when he looked at me, which set my heart fluttering in my chest. It was hard not to smile. But I played it cool. Well, I tried to. Seeing him like that, his shirt off, remembering the way his skin felt underneath my hands. I was probably three shades of red in my cheeks. I may be only a natural auburn, but we can blush just as badly as a full fledge redhead.

Having to get up early the next morning, I went up to shower and try to sleep. The hot day had turned into one of those hot, sticky summer nights. I heard Jake finally come up around midnight as I was still tossing and turning, unable to drift off. He appeared at my door and walked in. He didn't say a word, just leaned over, and started kissing me. Clothes were quickly discarded as a different heat took over both of us. This time it was different, a lot different.

He was too eager to be inside of me and kept trying to force it. He put me into different positions, mimicking the ones he had seen in his on-line porno, which he must have been watching after his parents went to bed and before coming upstairs. I went along, half out of my own ignorance and inexperience and half out of wanting to please him. Sweat was dripping off him like rain, soaking us both. I didn't mind that, found it sexy, because it was him and I told him so. It was such a hot night, and I no longer even had a fan in my room. The motor had burned out.

When he still couldn't get in me, he started touching me, trying to pull me open with his fingers. Last time he was gentle and tender, wanted to please me. This time he was rough and almost brutal, cold. After the first initial kisses, he didn't even do that anymore. No wonder my body wasn't being aroused enough. As I was starting to respond to his touches, he stopped and tried forcing himself into me again. When he felt the tip go in, he thrust the rest in hard and fast. I screamed in pain. I felt a popping inside me followed by a tear, like I had been ripped right open.

I switched. The alter who came out told him, "It's okay. I knew there would be some pain." Then she went right back inside.

This must have freaked Jake out or the fact that I really was a virgin did. Because he jumped up off me, off the bed, and started looking for his pajama bottoms. One of the littles came out then and was jumping around on her knees on the bed, laughing, helping Jake look for them, like it was a game they were playing. This made him even more anxious to get out of there. She finally found them tangled in my sheets on the floor. He snatched them and fled. Then, I switched again.

I was sore, very sore. I picked up my own pajamas and got them on. Jake was back at my door. I walked over there. He looked dark in the gloom of the hallway and I could feel this anger radiating off him like the heat had been. The dark side of him. I was scared. He told me that everyone knew about what had happened between us that other morning. Sally had told Vicky when she had gone down to Beloit to drop Alex off with his dad and visit some friends. Well, that explained why Jake's dad had been watching us like that on Saturday and why Jake had been so "busy" all weekend.

I started to shake. I told him, "I didn't mean to tell her. I was just so upset when you had said that you didn't remember and I needed someone to talk to. I thought she was my friend."

He was so angry. I started to cry. Then he told me, more like threatened me, "Do not tell anyone about this, especially not Sally or my parents."

I told him, "I won't. I am really sorry. I didn't mean to tell." Then he turned and walked back to his room.

I sat down on my bed, feeling sick, hurting so bad physically, emotionally. I felt so dirty and ashamed. I went and took a hot shower and scrubbed my skin raw. I was up crying for the rest of the night. I knew Jake could hear me crying. I didn't care.

When it was time to go downstairs and wait for Vicky to drop off Claire, I was scared. I didn't know what Vicky would say, how she would react to me. She has quite a temper when she is upset and had said hurtful things to me on occasion before. With something like this....

When she dropped Claire off she didn't say anything. It was like any other morning. I must have looked a wreck. I don't know how I got through that day. It hurt just to walk. I was hunched over like the Hunchback of Notre Damn. It even hurt so bad to go to the bathroom I would cry. No one said anything to me. Jake that afternoon was talking to someone on the phone and said that he was going to have nothing more to do with her. The "her", I assumed he meant, was me. Another blow.

After another day passed I was able to walk a little better, but then I started to bleed bad. I grew weaker and weaker. By Friday, I couldn't get out of bed. I lost 10 lbs overnight I bled so heavily. I had had heavy bleeds like this a couple of times before. I was afraid to tell anyone, to call Lynn, to go to the hospital. I didn't want Jake to get into trouble. He was 19 after all, a grownup in the eyes of the law, and had been sexually active since he was 16. The state of my body, the injury when I tore, the record of my emotional and mental problems and being treated for them, it just didn't look good for Jake. Even if I had consented to sex, I didn't consent to being hurt like that or treated like I was afterwards. I doubted anyone would believe that I wasn't forced. So, I didn't tell. Stupid, now to look back on it, but that was my reasoning at the time.

Jake knew how sick and weak I was. He passed my door Saturday and looked in on his way out to go to Beloit for a concert. I was very pale and could barely move. He didn't say anything, not to me, not to his parents. He just left with two friends of his to go stay the night over at Sally's house.

A few days later when I was starting to get my strength back, I found out not only had he spent the night there at her house, he stayed in her bed. Not even one week after leaving mine. He claimed to his parents that nothing happened. Nice. Whatever. He had claimed nothing had happened between the two of us either. But they bought it, hook, line, and sinker. He was their "baby boy" after all.

When Jake's parents did finally talk to me, they said that I had made everything up. That nothing had happened between me and him. I must have just dreamed it. Yeah, I dreamed getting torn up and bleeding so heavy I couldn't get out of bed. I even said that to Jake's dad, James, but he still insisted that I just dreamed it all. Ummm...I think I do know the difference between being awake and dreaming. Even vivid dreams can be distinguished from reality. I was "crazy", but not that crazy, people.

Esther sent me an e-mail accusing me of faking my DID. That my therapists knew it and I was just refusing to admit to my age. Oh, and I was stalking her son. How can you stalk someone you live with and had known for like 6 years by that time? Why would I lie and fake any of this anyways? I mean it sent my world, which wasn't perfect but manageable, into utter chaos. This greatly upset me as you can imagine. Words and accusations to hurt me as much as she could adding to my already considerable pain. The truth didn't matter. The truth didn't matter at all.

I finally told my therapists, Lynn and Louise, what had happened. They were concerned for my safety and insisted I move out of there as soon as I could. Both also told me that they in no way thought I was faking my disorder and Esther was out of line telling me that. With the confidentiality policy between patient and doctor or therapist, they would never have discussed my condition with her like that anyways. I started to seriously look for an apartment. The events that happened after would make it even more urgent that I leave.

I confronted Jake one night, told him we needed to talk. I was honest with him about how I felt about what he did to me, how he had treated me. How his family was treating me. He sat there denying still that he had done anything, that he had ever even been attracted to me. His eyes, his whole face told me he was lying and that he knew I was not buying it at all, frustrating him further. I cried and I got mad, very mad. It wasn't fair for me to be punished and treated like I had done something wrong, when I hadn't. It was something both of us did. I did not dream it. I told him how he had injured me. How could I have dreamt that up? I didn't do it to myself. When denying it didn't work any longer, he changed the subject.

Jake told me that Sally would be coming up to visit, though she was afraid to because she was afraid I would attack her. Me, attack her! I have never attacked anyone in my life. That was ridiculous. She was the one with the temper, who wanted revenge against her x-boyfriend when he broke up with her, threatening to trash his car and all kinds of stuff. For her to be afraid of me was utterly ridiculous, absurd, laughable. Then he told me that she would be sharing his room, his bed, and she was thinking of moving in. Talk about putting salt in an open wound.

Later that night when I was downstairs, I asked Esther, with Vicky standing there too, why she hadn't asked me what had happened. Why she had just listened to what Sally had said. All they had done was ask Jake, and of course he denied it. I asked her why when I was so weak, didn't anyone check on me. Her answer was that she thought I just needed, wanted to be alone for a few days. Jake heard all this from the basement stairs. I know because he came and stood in the room as his mom left to go back to her bedroom. He had a look of such sadness in his eyes. Maybe he was sorry for lying, for treating me like that. Maybe I just imagined the sadness and he really didn't care at all how much he hurt me. I will never know.

When Sally came up to visit for a week, she did indeed stay in Jake's room, in his bed. Even though he was staying in a tiny room, next to mine, until what would be his room on the other side of the bathroom was finished. That room was still a mess with only the sheet rock just done.

I stayed away from them both as much as possible. I slept with headphones on so I wouldn't hear them through the heat vent. Every opportunity she could, Sally would put on a display for me, kissing him, sitting close to him. She kept him up until 2 or 3 in the morning even though he had to get up early to go to work, so he wasn't sleeping much at all. She would make comments and remarks, subtle barbs. It was not an easy week to get through, not at all. Somehow, I survived it.

I talked to Todd. I just needed confirmation that I still had one friend left in the world. I didn't tell him what had happened, just that I was betrayed by both Jake and Sally. Being Jake's best friend I didn't want him to get caught in the middle. I told him that I had thought of asking him to beat Jake up for me, when I was so angry. He said that he and Jake had made a pact when they became friends that they would never fight over a girl. Though if Todd knew what Jake had done and how he had treated me, maybe he would have broken that pact. Anyways, Todd told me he was still my friend and still cared about me. He would even help me to move when I found a place.

*** *** ***

When I was reading through the journals written at this time, I realized that there was a lot I had forgotten. From June well into July I was suffering from depression and other emotional waves. Often I did not feel well. Jake was aware of this and I think it possible he used it. Depression really makes you feel cut off, alone, even more needy for affection, for connection to another human being. Everything is exaggerated.

I had been attempting to forge other relationships, to socialize. There were several males who expressed a mild interest in me, that never went anywhere beyond some e-mails and light flirting. Still it was a start. Though the "failures" added to my depression and did not help my poor self-image any. Jake was aware of this too.

Since I had been in the hospital, Jake and I had not even hugged. We had lived under the same roof for 3 years and I had done nothing inappropriate. Even those times he hugged me or held my hand could have been the gesture of one friend to another, of caring. I was resolved and cared about him as a friend, a good friend at this time, nothing more. Even if some of his other behaviors at times, confused and frustrated me. I appreciated it when he acted like a friend and mourned the loss of that friendship when he was cold and distant.

It is more obvious to me as I look back now, that I was taken advantage of. I was played by someone with more experience, who was well aware of my emotional state, for his own purposes. He then used my emotional state to "deny" it happened at all, making it all, my problem to deal with. He acted as if he was in no way at fault or responsible to any degree for his part in this mess. Nor did anyone point it out to him, except for me.

When Jake first approached me that summer morning, he was already thinking, planning on asking someone else to go out with him, Sally. She was someone who his family had long been pushing and longing for him to hook up with. His intentions towards me were poor all along. He had planned how he was going to use me, whether for the one time or continually for however long he chose to. My emotional state and innocence and inexperience really made me vulnerable to his mind games.

I did not want to believe it, of course. Even now, it is difficult to accept, but I must.

CHAPTER FIVE

As I stated on the dedication page, I am writing this in the first person even though it is different alters who have experienced these things. It is easier to write that way and easier to read. I also need to own these things, which have happened, both the good and the bad. Writing in the first person, saying I, instead of she or we, helps us to own it. It is no longer what happened to her, but to me. After all each of these alters is a piece of me, this body, this mind. It is like the different parts of a rose, all the different petals, the stem, and the thorns. Or rather, as one little likes to think of us, we are a rose garden.

Another reason to write in the first person is we cooperate as a group. Our own little community inside who can support, encourage, and comfort. The littles need no longer deal with their traumas all on their own. The bigs can help all to get out, experience life, grow, and heal from those traumas and change how those traumas shaped us as an individual and influenced our view of the world. We can change how we react and interact with the world.

It really is like having an inner community. Each alter, each piece of Rose, has her own unique experiences, attitudes, feelings, memories, abilities, talents, interests, similar to any community. What one may fear another embraces. Where one is weak another is strong. Where one is wise another is foolish.

Each alter is also physically different. Not all of my alters have arthritis or the same kind of arthritis. Not all alters have chronic depression. Some alters have a higher normal body temperature, some lower. Some alters have problems with their heart and blood pressure going high so that they become dizzy and even have passed out. Some alters love spicy food and can eat jalapeños, for others those kinds of foods upset their stomach. My hormone levels fluctuate. I have to be careful what medicines I take, even just for pain. What is a necessary dosage for a big would be too much medicine for a little.

I have to always keep in mind whatever I do that I am little, middle, and big all at the same time. What effects one could affect all. Not just in regards to diet, exercise, and medications, but also in regards to relationships and other interactions with the outside world.

Most of the littles and middles were born of traumas and the effects those traumas had on my psyche. The bigs were born out of necessity, to be able to engage in a strange new world. Some people look at the birth date and identity that I have had to use since I was a baby and say that I am such and such an age. They have expectations, prejudices, and a "box" they put me in to. They cannot understand that I do not fit and can never fit that box. No matter how much time has passed according to the Earth's travels around the sun, for me not so much time has passed. I am not that age. I will never "catch up" and match that age. Even Lynn had a hard time dealing with the fact there is no insider who matches that time span. I just didn't fit the other DID clients she had had, my whole dynamic was different.

I am but a young woman just starting out in life. I am struggling like any normal person in their late teens and early twenty's to find out who they are, what the world is like, their place and purpose in that world. Having a traumatic past makes that difficult to do.

Lies and programming from those traumas, the very stresses from living in that kind of environment for so long, wired my brain in a certain way. I know only how to survive in a highly traumatic environment, not a healthy one. My normal growth, in all areas, was stunted, put on hold for long periods of time, not for days but months, maybe even years. That includes physical, emotional, social, spiritual, and mental growth. The traumas extended over several growth stages, from infancy to school-age, only slowing down as I reached my teenage years, or what should have been my teen-age years. Each alter stuck at a certain age or stage of life. Not so difficult then at 13 to die in a sense, to continue going on with the motions of living, while not really being there at all, not engaging in life, not growing further.

One of the common symptoms or difficulties of being DID, or multiple is memory blanks. I have referred to my past feeling like postcards from someone else's life. These postcards are images or facts concerning certain things that happened, people encountered. They are not memories, though. These little postcards are all I have of my past, except for the few memories that I have recovered. Some of those postcards are from what other people told me happened to them, not from any memory any of us insiders have. I needed to have a past, as all people do, and since these were the memories of siblings I was raised with, I claimed them.

I call it traumatic amnesia, these memory blanks. I picture it as a huge black hole, which sucked everything in when I was a child and it still wants to suck new memories in. All of them were then stored in a dark locked vault I cannot access. I was left with a fact file. A cabinet into which the basics of things I need to know are put and more added as the need for certain information comes up. I do not know who controls it. It is from the vault that trauma memories are unleashed when I am ready to process through it. I say unleashed, because like a rabid dog, they come upon me and knocked me flat on my ass, biting and clawing. Not all at once of course, that would only created new breaks. It is always in pieces. Emotional waves. Body memories, with physical sensations running through me. Just knowing something happened as a new fact is added to the fact file.

To complicate matters, as if I need any more complications, the degree of stress I was under when living in the midst of all these traumas, prohibited my ability to record new memories and to access them later. Each alter who experienced multiple traumas may not have been able to recover from the stress of one trauma before experiencing another one. It is quite possible that the traumas were recorded at the time as one huge trauma instead of separate trauma experiences, a mega trauma so to speak.

It is much better then to take it in pieces. The stress from one trauma is great enough, the stress from a mega-trauma would be unbearable. I would loose all sanity and perhaps even my life under such a weight. Being recorded in such a way, I may never know just all that was done to me, or by how many. The little that I do know is hard enough to live with. It is only pieces of those pieces I have revealed in these pages. Enough to give the idea of the things I have experienced and how that shaped me and influenced my interactions with the people I encountered during the particular time frame of this part of my story.

My self-esteem and view of myself as a person was created and warped by these traumas and the way I was treated by those around me. Talents and abilities lay hidden within or utilized only on a minimal basis. I learned not to attract attention, attention equaled pain. I was nothing, a Nobody, a nameless face in a crowd. I was what people needed and wanted me to be with no knowledge of who I really was. As I said in an earlier chapter, I lived only a façade.

Coming from a traumatic environment and my brain wired for survival in that kind of world, I still respond to things and people in the same way. A small put down, even one done in a joking manner, I can react to like it is a big putdown. I am vulnerable to different kinds of abuses, from people who no one would consider abusive in any way and would not normally treat others in that way, because of my reaction to things. Jake and his family are one such example. No one would ever believe that they were abusive or capable of such behavior.

I sometimes feel like I have some neon sign over me that says, "Hey, it is okay to abuse this one. It is what she was made for." That is the truth I learned when I was very young, ingrained with every punch and kick and rape. Sure, I know now that it is a lie. No one deserves, or is created, to be abused in any way. I struggle each day to reshape my view of self and how I react and interact with the world. I work hard to understand myself, the whys of my being this way. As I do, I grow less vulnerable, less a Nobody, and more a worthwhile person. The mirror I see myself through is cracked and warped, but bit by bit is growing straighter and clearer.

Going through a breakdown and the trauma memories and emotional waves during the time I lived with Jake and his family was like being again in that environment I grew up in. I was in survival mode. I was highly sensitive to everything. Some of their reactions to me and what was happening, I know were born out of frustration and confusion. All things were heightened, including those feelings I had for Jake. I thought I was in love when really I was in love with love. A normal way for any teenage girl to feel and react, compounded by a deep need to be loved and belong somewhere. I could not really love him or anyone until I learned to love myself.

The little steps I had started taking before that experience with Jake that one weekend, were my learning to love myself. The traumatic events of that one night and what followed, were a deep blow. I was tumbled backwards. If it were not for Todd sticking by me, I would have tumbled even further back. With the help of my two therapists, I was able to pick myself up and do what I needed to do to free myself and enter a new environment.

CHAPTER SIX

At first, I looked at staying in Berlin. Change is a very scary thing for most people, doubly so for anyone with a highly traumatic past and who had just gone through another traumatic experience. I was familiar with Berlin after living there for almost two years, though it feels like longer than that.

I encountered two problems with that. First, I had a very limited budget. If I could afford the rent, the winter utilities I could not afford. I also did not have anything to put down towards a security deposit. I could not wait to move until I had saved up enough, not when I would need what equaled to or was more than one month's income. Then there would be the rent on top of that. It would take months to save that kind of money, if at all.

The second problem was Jake. He had started using drugs. I did not want to believe it at first. He knew what drugs had done to his sister, Vicky. He had always been against using them, now he was. I knew, however, it was true. Having lived in the city, in the neighborhood I had, there was a lot of drug use. I was well aware of the signs and symptoms. Some of the main traumatic abuses of my past were done under the influence of alcohol and drugs. I had double the reason to be concerned. I question whether or not this was even a new thing with him or if Jake might have been using during that time he was drinking back before we moved north and right afterwards.

One night I was out with the dogs when Jake came home from being out with his friends. His eyes were all huge, dark, and shiny. The very way he walked was different. He was flirty with me, looking me over as a guy would any good looking girl. Now ordinarily that would not have bothered me coming from him, but this was after what had happened between us, after I confronted him about it and he denied even being attracted to me. If he had been using drugs that weekend…if he had been using for some time…that would help explain the change in how he looked at me. How he could under the influence of those drugs and spurned on by the pornography treat me the way he did that night. That he could do so again. Especially, now that I was no longer a virgin and no one would believe me if he did. After all, they didn't believe me now. He could deny all he wanted and get away with it, putting me in a dangerous position.

He did not believe that I was a virgin until that night, maybe not even then. He knew I had been raped when young, though not how young. How then could I be a virgin? Rape is not sex. It is an assault attacking the sexual organs and one's sexuality. It is like being shot or knifed or beat up. Rape as a small child certainly cannot be counted as sexual experience. I hadn't even had my first kiss until just a few months prior to being with Jake that weekend. It has also been recorded that that little bit of flesh inside of us females that is "popped" our first time, can grow back if not sexually active for years and all those muscles tighten back up. It also can be torn by horseback riding or receiving some traumatic blow to that area, say from a bicycle accident where you land hard on the stabilizer bar. I most likely also have scar tissue from being raped so very young.

I defiantly was still a virgin until that particular night. Not one of those teaser virgins either, females who do everything sexually except for vaginal intercourse. I really was a virgin in every aspect, until Jake. Sometimes I wish it hadn't happened, not like that anyways. Not exactly a good "first time" for someone who has already been hurt more than enough.

It was therefore vital that I get out of that house as soon as possible. When Lynn suggested an apartment building she knew of in Green Lake, I, at first, wouldn't consider it. Moving to a whole new town that meant starting over. I didn't know if I could do it. As I thought it over though, I realized that putting some distance between Jake and I was a very good idea. I no longer knew what he was capable of and that frightened me.

Starting over would also mean new opportunities. I would be my own girl. I could do what I wanted to, go where I wanted to. I would be able to take the time I needed for my healing. I might be able to make friends, not just online, but real world friends. That was exciting.

I made an appointment to see an apartment. There were four empty at the time so I was able to choose which one I wanted. The security deposit was lower than other places I had looked at and the manager said I could pay it in two installments. The rent being 30% of my income meant that I would easily be able to pay all my bills and buy food and even spoil myself once in awhile. Now what girl wouldn't like that? I filled out the paper work right away. Within the week I found out that the apartment was mine. Given my particular situation, the manager did all he could to rush the process.

Part of me is very organized. When I had decided I was going to move out, I started going through all my things, deciding what I wanted to keep and what I didn't. I made a list of all the things I would need to do. There was changing the bank account from a joint to a single checking account. Change of address cards from the post office. Picking up moving boxes. Setting up phone service and purchasing a phone. Finding someone to help me move. Todd said he would help, just let him know when. All the other little details you have to take care of when moving. After moving so often, I knew what I needed to do.

Esther helped me pack my things from the kitchen. Vicky gave me a couple of decorative items that she had been given by an x-boyfriend she had recently broken up with. Since the apartment had been empty for a while, I was able to start moving in my things. I didn't have much so it only took two trips with James' car to move my boxes and other little things over. Todd wasn't able to help. His dad wouldn't let him borrow the truck.

I spent my last night in that house in Berlin sleeping on my mattress and box spring on the floor. I was so excited. I was doing it. I was finally going to live on my own again. I kept going over things in my mind making sure I didn't forget anything.

Jake's parents would come pick me up when we had to travel to Milton for the appointment with Louise, who was also Esther's therapist and had been for a long time. That was how they got me to start going to see her. They were already traveling down there twice a month. We just had to have appointments on the same day back to back. No problem. I watched Claire and Alex, who had to come with us since Vicki was working, while Esther was in her appointment. Then she would watch the kids while I was in my appointment. A pretty good arrangement.

I said I could still help watch Claire and Alex once in a while. Claire was the saddest to see me move out. She felt like she was loosing her only friend. She would be starting preschool soon though and would make other friends. I would miss her too and her brother of course.

September arrived, the start of Labor Day weekend. It was a bright warm day that year of 2004. I had notified my new manager, Fred* (short for Federico*), when I would start staying overnight in my apartment. Vicki didn't have to work that day, but Jake and his parents had just moved an

Aunt down to Louisiana the past week and were still sore. I wasn't even sure I wanted Jake's help at all. I was still scared of him somewhat. I had reason to be didn't I? So moving would be more difficult and I might have to allow him to help his father with my big stuff, like my bed. Yeah, the thought of him carrying my mattress after what he did to me on it gave me the willies.

The day went by slowly. I helped take care of Claire and Alex. I made sure my old room was clean. That I didn't forget anything in the bathroom. The only big things that needed to be moved were my bed and my two chairs. That was really the only furniture I had, except for a dresser I did not really need anymore and two bookcases, one that was being used for all the kids books and the other one I didn't want to take. I decided to move light and take only what I needed and really wanted.

The day rolled into late afternoon. I asked when I could be taken over to my apartment. They wanted me to wait another day or two. I did not want to wait. I felt like if I didn't go that day I wouldn't be able to and suspected it was just a way to keep me there and not let me go. I began to cry and said I want to go home. I hadn't even been there one night and already felt it was my home, not the place where I had been living with Jake and his family.

They continued trying to convince me to wait, but I would not. James gave in. I packed the little bit I had left into the car, the two cushions for my chairs and one chair in the trunk. My bed would have to wait for another day, though I did take all my bedding. I didn't care. I was going home.

When I got to my new apartment, I opened up both windows. One is in the living room and the other in the bedroom. I then started to unpack my things and organize it. It was fun deciding which drawer to put what in, which cabinet for dishes, which for foodstuffs. I made a little bed on the floor, carpeted nicely and padded, with my bedding.

It did not take very long. I really did not have that much stuff as I said.

Tia had an inner conference and told them all that this was our place. We could decorate as we wanted to reflect ourselves. The furnishings we could add as we found pieces that we liked. We didn't have to rush to fill it up. The possibilities were endless as long as we stayed within the guidelines outlined in the lease. She said she was proud of everyone for handling this move and doing all that they needed to do, even if they felt afraid or nervous. That made everyone happy.

For days, even months, after moving in I would look around my apartment and see it as if I was seeing it for the first time and was not sure where I was. Then I would hear Tia telling the alter who was looking through my eyes, that this is our apartment. A strange thing to have happen, but when you are a multiple those kinds of things happen all the time.

The first friend I made here was Gail. She took me around Green Lake in her car, showing me where everything was. I had already been to the local library many times as well as the little grocery store, since that was where Jake and his father worked. Then there was that horrendous time sitting in front of the police station that July day a few years before and the trip to the courthouse. Times I would rather forget. As for anything else in town, I had no clue. Being shown around like that helped me to not be as scared to venture out and explore on my own. Knowing a few places already helped with the Agoraphobia, so I was not trapped inside as I had been after so many other moves.

As the months passed, I met and got to know some more of my neighbors. I would sit down in the lounge during the day and read or watch TV. On Sundays, a group of us would watch the football games. One neighbor got a kick watching some of my littles and their reactions to the game. It was not uncommon to see me walking around carrying a stuffed animal, but no one treated me as if it were very strange to do so. Several of them had themselves a collection of stuffed creatures. If anything, it was a good conversation starter.

I involved myself in the activities and things going on in the building. There were monthly tenant association meetings in the community room. As well as potluck dinners, where tenants signed up a few weeks prior to the event so everyone knew what was being brought. It was a good way to meet neighbors and socialize.

The community room is this nice sized room with its own kitchen. There are several long tables and one small round table for games or puzzles, kept in a closet and free for any tenant to use when they would like to. A bookcase sits near this round table with books tenants can borrow. The Senior Meal Site is held there four times a week. The room, decorated with window clings and other things for the seasons and holidays, feels warm, friendly, inviting.

Jake's parents became upset with me one day, because I could not baby sit Claire and Alex on their wedding anniversary. I had my initial appointment with a new chiropractor and Lynn was coming with me to help me through it. With her busy schedule and not knowing how long the appointment would take, I couldn't just cancel it. It was something important I needed to do for me. I was sorry, but it wasn't right for them either to ask me at the last minute and expect me to drop everything. I was starting to finally have a life of my own.

One day shortly after that, on our bi-monthly trip to Milton, the behavior of Jake's parents towards me was cold and unfriendly. I felt very uncomfortable and got the impression they no longer wanted to take me with them down there. They never came out and said it though. I was upset when I got home that night. Wondered what I would do. Gail rescued me, offering to drive me down there herself. She enjoys road trips. I would pay her for the gas and a little extra. What a lifesaver.

I stopped going to the little grocery store too. A couple of times I went there while Jake was working. Once, to pick up a few things and once, to drop off with him some papers for his mom, since for a couple of months after I had moved out their phone was still in my name. I didn't mind at first, until I received a phone bill with $30.00 worth of long distance calls that were just Jake's calling Sally. Then there was his local toll calls to Princeton and Ripon to his friends there. He wasn't my friend anymore but I was responsible to pay for his calls. Yeah right. Dream on. I was so glad when Esther was finally able to straighten things out and I no longer had to worry about it.

Oh and there was the time I went in to the store with Claire when I baby sat her at my apartment, (We had a blast by the way, her and I, playing at the park and watching a movie.), just to say hi. But with the attitude I was now getting from Jake's parents and Jake's behavior that summer, I was just not comfortable going anymore. I started doing all my shopping in a nearby town. That turned out to be a good thing anyways, because that little store shut down before too long.

I went to the library three times a week. Just to get out and about, which helped my Agoraphobia from taking a major hold again. I would pick up movies and books. The movies ensured that I would have to get out at least once a week, no matter how I was feeling. I was also able to check my e-mails and chat with some on-line friends I had made as well as Todd. Most were just casual that I talked to now and then, but a few I talked to regularly.

Someone in the apartment building got the false impression that I had all these boyfriends kept on a string, just because there were several guys that I communicated with on the computer. Please. Talking to a guy about doctors or general stuff doesn't make him a boyfriend.

Sometimes they just needed someone to talk to, to listen. I talked to plenty of females too, does that make them "girlfriends"?

You see how ridiculous some people are. This particular individual would not let go of it and would cause some trouble for me later on. I sure wasn't going to let one person's "opinions" stop me from socializing though. Most people found me warm, friendly, kind, helpful, and nice. That is what matters, right.

It was so much fun meeting people from all over the world through the wondrous technology of the computer and internet. We all have something in common no matter where we are from and our individual cultures. There were a few wankers of course. You know the types of males I mean, (well some females too exist who are the same way), the ones who start IM-ing (Instant Message, like talking real time with your fingertips) you when you are on-line asking personal questions, usually with sexual connotations. I really hate that. They just have no respect for themselves or anyone else. Please. As if.

I signed up to a website for making friends. There was a profile of course, where you put a little about yourself, interests, hobbies, all that, as much or as little as you want. There's a place for pictures. A public journal anyone on the site could read, which was fun to write in about whatever. You could send messages to others at the site or a message to all your friends at once with the bulletin board.

Best part was that there was a little safety built into the site. Only those you were networked to could send you messages. The network was made up of those you add to your friend list and those on their lists as well as the people in the groups you joined. The groups were a bulletin board type of messaging about a particular topic, like music, games, movies, relationships. You could "ignore" anyone you didn't want to contact you. Friends were added only by mutual consent and could be deleted from your list at any time. Pretty cool, huh. I thought so too.

A couple of people I met there became very good friends. One was Suha*, a girl in England who was originally from the Middle East. She had actually studied about multiple personalities in school and realized from reading my journal entries that I was one. She was very excited to meet and talk with someone with the disorder. We discovered we had a lot in common, including abusive pasts and struggles with the here and now and our self-image. You know it is far easier to impart wisdom to others to help them than to use it to help yourself. It is true, yet all the lies seem to have such a louder voice and make that truth harder to believe when it comes to your self.

The other was Dante. I read his profile one day just browsing the site. He had a comment written there that he bet there wasn't anyone "weirder" out there than him. So I sent him a message and said oh yes there was, me. Turns out, Dante was my brother. Okay so he is a cosmic twin brother, but still family and my lighthouse when the storms rage that guides me home. My soul, I would be so lost without. He understands me like no one else does and we often go through the same things at the same time. Just a fluke, a happenstance, coincidence, divine hand, whatever you want to call it, but the best thing that had happened to either of us in a long time and at a time when we most needed it.

Dante is the only family I have, though I think of some around the apartment building as Granny or Uncle or Aunt. Blood does not make you family, especially in an age where divorce is cheap and too common and siblings are a mix of full, half, and step brothers and sisters. No, family is a connection of the heart and mind and will. The acceptance of another person completely, faults and all, loving no matter what. Dysfunction is a lack of connectedness. Where you must "earn" love and acceptance and can loose it at anytime for any reason. To have that one person who accepts me fully as I am is more precious than anything else this universe has to offer. It cannot be bought or sold or lost or earned, but is a precious gift, given freely.

CHAPTER SEVEN

I remembered more fragments of my birth family. My mothers long auburn hair with soft large curls. I used to play with them with my tiny fingers, when they did not ache from the arthritis. I remembered her voice when she sang and discovered a modern singer whose voice sounded much like hers. What a comfort that was on hard days. I heard her voice in my own singing at times. Sometimes I missed her so much, needed her so much. I weep for all those things that we never got to know or experience as mother and daughter.

The woman in that very first flashback I had had was my mother. For some reason the man had barged into the house and she fought to protect her family. She died that day. The very last image I had, as the man carried me out of the house, was of her slumped up against the wall, not moving, her eyes dull. The sparkle in them I had known, gone.

I remembered my father. I saw him as a reflection in a mirror. His hair was black and slightly coarse. His eyes had a greenish hue. His skin was medium beige. Fred, the manager of the apartment building, reminded me a lot of my father in looks. They could have been brothers. Fred is Hispanic. It was entirely possible that my father was also Hispanic and I therefore was too, at least half that is.

Rosilita, the smallest alter, hears Spanish all the time. She is too little yet to speak it and does not know what the words mean, but she loves the sound of it. She has told me that my real name, the one mother and father gave to me when I was born, is Rosilita Maria. I was named after my paternal grandmother Rosa. I look like Grandma Rosa, Rosilita has said, when my hair is dyed black, from a picture she had seen of Grandma taken when Grandma was young.

One day while watching Oprah, I remembered what had happened to my father. It was after that huge tsunami devastated so many different places in 2005. Her show was about what had happened to the people in those countries afterwards. They showed a man forced to kneel in the street by another man who was wearing a military uniform. The soldier shot him. That triggered me so bad I had to leave the room.

I shook and cried and could hear little Rosilita saying, no, screaming in my head, "Daddy! Daddy!" It was the same day my mother had died. I had seen my father shot. Oh, my. Poor baby, to have had to witness that....Oh my...and on the same day as Mommy.

I remembered my sister. Her hair was black like Daddy's. She was five years old at the time when I lost my family. She was sitting at a table in the sunlight streaming through the window next to her. There was another kid sitting next to her. Perhaps it was a friend visiting for the day, or a cousin. Because of the brightness of the sunlight, I could not see my sister's face. I was being held at the time, for I was looking downwards at her. I do not know what happened to her, if she was killed or also taken away.

Soon after moving here to Green Lake, I started taking walks down to the lakeshore. One morning I walked down to the beach with my headphones on and sat at the end of a pier they had there. I looked out over the waves. I began to feel slightly dizzy and like I was moving up and down with the waves. One of the piers along the lakeshore actually does move up and down. However, the one I was sitting upon was stationary.

Images formed in my mind's eye and there were sounds beneath the music playing in my ears. I saw my father and sister playing in the waves, laughing and splashing each other. I could feel the warmth of my mother's body as she held me close. Then I felt the coolness of the water on my feet and on the front of me as the waves lapped against us. I could distinctly feel the difference between mother's warmth and the cool water. Gentle tears ran down my cheek.

It was Indian Summer when my parents were killed. Those bright, sunny, and warm days. Leaves rustling in the strong breezes. The air with a tinge of coolness to it. I counted back six months from when Indian summer usually appears, since that was my age at the time it happened. That would make me a spring baby, born sometime from late March to early May. The memory of playing in the water confirms that I was indeed born in the spring and that it had to be fall when I lost them. Another piece to my true identity so different from that "alias" I have had to live under for so long.

I do not know who the man was that robbed me of my family or why I was spared and taken away. I do not know where I was born, if it was even in this country at all. I know the military has something to do with it. For a long time I hated the military, any military. I thought of them as trained killers. My opinion changed when Jake was in JROTC and I learned that that was not true. I was very proud of Jake and he looked so very handsome and confident in that uniform. It is possible my father had been in the military, stationed in another country when some insurrection or disturbance broke out and my family was attacked. It is possible my parents were missionaries or the country where I was born underwent some revolution or something. All I do know and may ever know is that my family was murdered and I was cast into hell, while they went up to heaven to be with Jesus.

There are a lot of things that I cannot explain and will never know the whole truth of. I ended up with Robert and Sandra Weiss. I was given the identity of a daughter of theirs who had recently died. My identity, my heritage, was stripped from me. I was injected with hormones and things to help me grow faster in order to fit better into the roll I was being forced to play. My eye color, hair, and skin tone I had inherited from my mother. It was close to the little girl I was replacing. I was intelligent and quickly learned my alphabet and numbers and everything that a preschool/kindergarten age child would know. It is amazing the capabilities of the human mind. Whoever did these things to me knew what they were doing.

Why do it? How was it even possible? How could they get away with it? Who were they? Why not just have me adopted? Why go through all that trouble? How long did this process actually take? What happened to that little girl? How did she die? I do not know. It seems straight out of a Twilight Zone episode doesn't it?

What is even more bizarre is that a few months before I moved from Berlin I contacted as many schools, doctors, and hospitals that I could even slightly remember having been to. I was trying to piece my past together and find clues to who I was as well as documentation of the abuse, since so much of it is a big blank. I signed release forms so that they had my permission to send me a copy of my file, under the Freedom of Information Act, with full name, social security number, birth-date, year frame included.

Envelopes started to arrive. There was Lois's original birth record and a record of the labor. *(Lois was the girl's name who I replaced. Lois Sarah. It is a pretty, old-fashioned name, after Sandra's own mother. Sandra's mother died when Sandra was about nine years old. That name never suited me and always felt wrong somehow.)* It was a regular uncomplicated labor. A healthy baby girl. No birth marks, which is interesting since I happen to have a small birthmark on my upper right thy just below my buttocks. It looks like a triangle with a lengthened point at the top, like the Eiffel Tower, and next to it a half circle sitting on the straight edge. It was smaller when I was heavier and I suppose it will change yet as I loose more weight.

Everything that I received was basic and very generic. It could have been information about any average girl in the United States. The most important records were the ones that could not be found or I was told did not even exist. Like the Social Services records in the county where I had lived most of that time. After Robert and Sandra divorced, Social Services had come over to the house several times for "inspections". My sisters (Sandra and Roberts two other daughters) and I had to sit up all nice and straight with a smile on our faces, wearing pretty dresses, as if everything was just hunk-dory. The house was spotless, when it was usually a disaster. A nice show to hide what was really going on there. Usually for these spot inspections, the house was cleaned by some teenagers who lived down the street and baby sat us once in a while.

The only indication anywhere of any problem was in a small school nurse notation indicating "shyness and emotional problems due most likely to parent's divorce". That was it! No breaks, no bruises, no records of emergency room visits except one where I had hit my head and received a concussion in the third grade. Not even the gynecological visits I had had that indicated a problem with my ovaries or the physical I had to have before I could start working in a day care where I had gotten a job. The clinics I had gone to for all that said that no one by that name had ever even been a patient there. I tried twice, making sure all the information was correct. Nada. Nothing.

How does this made sense? I have had breasts since I was 8. In fact, when I was 11 I was told I looked 16, when 13 told I looked 30. I started my periods at 13, for a few months at least, and then they stopped. At 16, a doctor after examining me told me my ovaries were immature. How could that be? I should have been a late bloomer then, not an early one. Is that an indication that my hormones were "monkeyed" with when I was very young? Clearly, something wasn't right. The doctor put me on some kind of hormone pill which doubled my breast size during the 6 months or so I was on it and made the periods so heavy I was weak and loopy in the head. Well, more loopy than normal. When the pills ran out, I didn't get them refilled. *(These ages are based on what age I was told I was, that false identity I was given. I may have been two or more years younger and of course I stopped "aging" at 13, so though the Earth still turned and went about the sun and time continued on, I in essence didn't. Wonder how that affected my physical condition?)*

Then at 19, I saw a different doctor at a different clinic, also no records existing. This doctor wouldn't say anything specific of course and paying it out of pocket as I was, he didn't do any tests to find out. He just told me that I most likely had ovarian cysts and that was what was making me so irregular. He told me that the chances of me having any children were slim and I might have to use a fertility drug. For a young woman, who wanted to be a mom and had taken care of other people's kids since 11 years old that was devastating news. I knew, just knew within me that I would never bear a child, that I could not. I sunk me into a depression and soon after, I was laid off from a job at a day care center, making the depression worse.

This second doctor put me on a different hormone medication, which also doubled my breast size yet again. Just great! I know small breasted women out there are so jealous, wishing they had bigger breasts. They don't know how lucky they are. Not only are there the stares and innuendoes from the male as well as female population, bad enough for someone like me who was so severely abused. There is also the back pain and strain on my neck and shoulder muscles as well as the difficulty buying clothes that fit, especially bras and swimsuits. I mean I have to buy jackets two sizes too big to make sure they can close and as for button up blouses, forget it.

How could those records not exist? How could there be no notations of mysterious bruises or the deep emotional problems associated with children who are suffering from child abuse? Did I hide all those bruises that well? Was I so quiet and average that no one took any notice of me at all? Did the DID and the need to keep my "secret" hide all the bruises and breaks under my skin so deep that there were none to be seen?

What about the arthritis in my hands? Where are those records? Juvenile arthritis is common after all. Did not the pediatrician I was taken to for shots and checkups notice anything? That specific clinic and doctor were long gone so I couldn't even attempt to get those records. I suspect that even if I knew where to look I would have received a letter stating that no such files exist for that person. No wonder I have had problems feeling real.

It makes me wonder who my real parents were. What happened to them, by whom? Why would someone need to go to all that trouble to change me, hide who I was, even what I had suffered while with the Weiss'? Or is the answer simply, that they could? Many bizarre and cruel things are done just because they can. Things done by individuals, organizations, and governments do so, because they have the power to, because the technology exists to do it. Too bizarre. Yet that is my reality.

The house where I associate the biggest portion of my abuses we call the bad magic house. It was a new house located in a subdivision between East Troy and

Mukwonago. The things that went on there that I remember and know from the fact file are beyond horrible. Abuses occurred not just from Sandra, but also from her endless stream of lovers.

One such incident that illustrates this, I remembered when Fenix emerged, or rather when Tia and Lolo found her. I was at an appointment in Lynn's office not long after my breakdown and ending up in the hospital. She was using a therapy technique with this bar of lights that I had to focus on. The lights flashed on and off in different patterns at different speeds controlled by her with a switch. I was to focus on the body sensations I had been having and the emotions I felt with those sensations. As I did so, I began to see and hear things that were not in the room around me, but in my own mind.

Tia and Lolo heard a little girl crying. It was coming from behind a brick wall. Tia picked up a heavy object and hit the wall with it as hard as she could. A hole opened up in the bricks. Tia looked through the hole and saw in the gloom a little girl huddled in a corner, very frightened. She told the little girl not to be afraid. They were going to help her. Then Tia went back to work on the bricks until she had opened up a hole big enough for someone to get through. Lolo decided that she had better be the one to go in and approach the little girl. She might be less frightened of another child, than of an adult. *(This was of course before Tia revealed to all of us that she was only 13 and not 23. Still even at only 13 she still looked like a grown up.)*

After Lolo talked a little to the girl, calmed her, then Tia entered the little room and helped guide her out. They took her to the safe house. The safe house is a cabin in the middle of deep woods with wolf guards and a hidden secret path. It is the place where all the alters live after coming out. A place only in my mind, built as we need it to be. Tia took her to a bedroom on the first floor, cleaned her up, and put her to bed underneath the comfy quilts we have there. It was later that Fenix picked her name and told Tia what had happened to her.

I was about eight years old. Sandra was calling me all kinds of terrible names and swearing at me. She was holding me up against a wall, her hands squeezing my arms hard. As she continued to scream these at me, she started beating me with her hands. I fell to the floor, curled into a ball, and she began kicking me in the hip and lower back. One of her lovers was sitting there watching.

When she was finished, she turned to him and told him it was his turn. He could do anything he wanted to me, anything at all. He started calling me names and beating on me, kicking me. Then he raped me. Sandra was sitting on her bed, laughing as she watched. When he was finished, they both left the room, leaving me there on the floor. They were high or drunk or both and staggered some as they left the room, laughing like that had been the greatest of fun.

I know that many more such experiences happened to me there in that house. Sometimes mixed with spiritual elements, as high they would play around with an Ouija Board. The house was supposedly built over an old graveyard. How much fun it was for them to have me terrorized by spirits even as I was by them.

Robert himself did not abuse any of us, least that I remember. His sin was in being silent and doing nothing to protect me or his other children. He often came home in the evening from work and found us locked in the basement, while Sandra and one of her lovers sat in the kitchen in bathrobes partying. We had been down there all day with nothing to eat. He made a very good wage as a machinist in a Milwaukee factory. Yet the house had little furniture and decorations. Even after living there for years, there were still no curtains on most of the windows. Toys and books were from his parents and a friend of Sandra's from her days growing up in Milwaukee.

Robert saw, knew what was happening there, maybe not all of it, but enough. Yet he said nothing, did nothing to protect us. His response was to get a second job so that he wouldn't have to come home at all except to sleep. One year, right before Christmas, Sandra kicked him out, or so she tells it. They divorced not long after and Robert remarried some woman he met while working at his second job, starting a new family with her. Leaving the rest of us he was to protect and care for to whatever fate would come in Sandra's hands.

Sandra denied being abusive or neglectful in any way. I was a "bad" child, a negative influence on the others, is what she told people. It was "tough love" when she gave me an eviction notice as a birthday present. I was only good to have around while she was able to collect child support and AFDC, which stopped once I turned 18. I was taking care of the house and yard all by myself and she was away all week with her boyfriend, who happened to be one of the men who had molested me when I was younger. He was even at that time under charges for molesting another girl, but she would not believe it and was mad at me for warning the kids in my neighborhood to stay away from him. I was only babysitting at the time at $2.00 per hour and she wanted me to fork over to her half my pay. I refused so I was kicked out. I was taking care of the house, buying my own food with my meager pay. Wasn't that enough? You'd think so.

Sandra took no responsibility for anything. Her focus was completely on her and how sick she was from this or that, how unappreciated and alone. She did whatever she could to elicit pity from others and believed all her own lies so much she did not even know anymore that they were lies. Anything kind Sandra did was a show for others to make them think she was a good mother and how hateful her children, how ungrateful.

I understand that she was a single mom. I understand that she lost her own mother very young and may have been abused by her father. I understand that she never loved Robert and he never loved her. It was a marriage of convenience so that they could escape their homes or problems. I understand that Sandra had emotional and perhaps mental problems, worsened no doubt by the drugs and alcohol. Then there was having multiple miscarriages, having one child die, and an "imposter" taking her place. I can see her as a hurt human being.

But that does not excuse it. I have forgiven her, meaning that I have taken back my power and refuse to hold bitterness and hate in my heart. I still feel angry sometimes when I remember. I feel it and let it go. Those I grew up with in that home did not suffer abuse to the degree I did, but they were also abused and severely neglected, used to hurt me and each other. They hate her. Hate her so much it robs them.

One of them herself is abusive to her children, reenacting what she herself had known. She learned and followed many of the behaviors and attitudes, which she saw Sandra do, and does not realize it. In fact, if you would tell her she is acting like her mother, she would deny it and become very upset. Her children have problems as a result, a continuation of the cycle of abuse.

The other has distanced herself completely. She lives in a world of money and possessions. Everything is a show to prove to the world that she is someone and good enough. The things she has, the fancy home, the high paying job, the masters degree are where she has put her worth as a person. It is a way to hide from her childhood and balm her wounds. I was an embarrassment to her because I did not have these things and did not want them. I was weak because of my problems, my fears. I was stupid because I did not have a college degree. I was lazy and wasting my life because I had chosen to take care of other people's children instead of work in a department store or some other "real" job.

I do not doubt that they saw the abuses done to me. The very witnessing of them and hearing the sounds of abuse would have left scars on them. I think that they also could sense that I was not really their sister. I did not really belong. Perhaps they in a way blame me for what was done to them. Not fair, but the whole situation wasn't fair was it?

CHAPTER EIGHT

The months passed here in Green Lake. Holidays arrived and went. Halloween. Thanksgiving. The first Christmas on my own again.

Fred accidentally put up the wrong tree in the lounge. So that he wouldn't have to put it away, he suggested I use it up in my apartment. When Christmas was over, I could put it back into the box. Save him some work. The neighbors cat, Chocolate, had to inspect the tree. Make sure I had it up okay and all. He came over quite frequently to make sure everything was okay around my apartment. The little ones liked looking at the lights. I bought presents, one for each group, (little, middle, and big) and a special present for Dianah, since December is her celebration month. It was a good Christmas and I did not feel as alone as I thought I would.

Different alters have different celebration months. Not really birthdays since aging is not according to days and months, but coming out and experiencing life and healing, learning, growing, connecting with the other insiders. A few have aged a little, those who have been out the most, healed the most. There is no linear line with me. It is a hodge-podge of intersecting lines and circles.

A multiple friend of mine illustrated it this way. Imagine time is a river. In some places it moves fast, in some places slow. This is where most people wade or swim. For those of us who are multiple though, we do not wade or swim the stream. For us there is a series of stepping stones. Each stone represents one of us, an alter. We hop from one stone to another, back and forth, in no obvious or chronological pattern. A stage of life, High School for instance, can be experienced by several alters, even very young ones. Some stones may be under the water and touch time, while others are high and dry in the sun.

I was asked by my therapists to make a timeline of my life. How can you make an accurate timeline when you experience things in such a hap-hazard way? I don't even have a real age. I am many ages all at the same time from 6 months old with the youngest, Rosilita to 20 with the oldest alter, Dianah. This is not how I am seen by others to be. But this is the way I experience and react to life and living. This is as much as I have been able to obtain in living. The farthest I have advanced in my growth as an individual.

That was the biggest difficulty I had encountered with Jake and his family. They looked only at some date on the calendar. They did not look at me. I had said that I had never been on a date much less a boyfriend. They refused to believe me. I just didn't remember it, they said. I must have. They refused to accept my truth.

I still run into that difficulty. I think I always will. It makes it harder to experience life and grow as a person when someone out there is constantly trying to push you to be who you are not. When you are not accepted as you are. It makes it hard to keep fighting and not give up, give in, and just go back to existing. It makes it harder to try something new, to approach a door of opportunity, and say why not take a chance. Like when a new young man moves into your apartment building.

His name was Jason*. He was 19, cute, and friendly. He seemed to me like a very nice guy, when Fred introduced me to him. A few days after that Jason surprised me. I still smile to think of it.

I was downstairs in the community room with Gail and Fred playing cards. Jason came into the building and Fred called him into the room. He sat down in the chair next to mine. We all chatted for a while. Then Gail said to Jason, "Don't you have a question you wanted to ask Rose." Jason turned to me and asked, "Will you be my girlfriend?"

His girlfriend! I blushed something fierce. I didn't know what to say. Was he was joking around or serious? Why would he even ask me that? He didn't even know me. I could tell by Gail's expression this was not the question she had expected him to ask. Fred got a kick out of my blushing and teased me good naturally.

I quietly told Jason, no. What else was I supposed to say? He was cute and all and a little shy. He seemed real sweet. But we had just met. I was still not over all that had happened with Jake. I wasn't certain of myself. I didn't think I could handle all the innuendoes and troubles that would be caused between who I really was and who people assumed and wanted me to be. Like with what had happened with Jake's family. That wound was still too raw.

That was in March of 2005. Over the next two months, my attitude towards Jason started to change. Sometimes he acted all player like. All big and bad and how could any female resist? That made me not like him much. Other times he was helpful and kind. As we talked and I got to know him a little, I realized the player act was just that, an act. It wasn't really him. I also noticed that "the act" was for other females. He wasn't like that with me.

One day he bent over the couch right next to where I was sitting, looking into the mirror hanging above the couch. I could smell his cologne and feel the warmth of his body only inches away from me. I liked it, liked it a lot. I was surprised by this response to him. I really didn't think I would ever be attracted to another guy. That was the reason Jake had had me all up in knots and confused. I had felt with him like I had never felt with any male before. Now here I was starting to feel these things again, with Jason. That thrilled and scared me. I wasn't sure I could take a chance. Not just on him, but on me.

Jason kept trying. He asked me several times to be his girlfriend, to give him a chance. He even asked me what kind of guy I was looking for. I politely said no. Fred told me that he was a nice guy who was looking for a nice girl he could have a relationship with. Problem was I wasn't sure I could handle a relationship. That was new ground for me. Jake and I had been really only friends. I was afraid to trust again, to open myself up to the possibility of more pain after how Jake and Todd had treated me.

A warm May afternoon, Jason and I were sitting out on the patio talking with another tenant. This tenant, Al, was being honest about how he had lived his life, the things he had done, which had led him to where he was now, a dying man only in his 40's. His life wasted in a pool of drugs and alcohol. That really touched Jason and made him think about the things he had also done. Where his life was or could go if he continued down the particular path he had been on. It touched me also, Al's openness and frankness. He did not lecture or say don't do it. He merely told a part of his story. *(Al is no longer with us, but he is remembered and that gift of truth he gave.)*

The conversation got around to me being a multiple. Both were not freaked out by it, but accepting. Jason even correctly guessed a couple of the names of my alters. Jason started joking around about me giving him a kiss. I told him no. I didn't feel comfortable doing that. Well, I wasn't very experienced was I? I kind of used Jake as an excuse and had been using him as an excuse to keep Jason back, to keep myself back. I still hadn't really dealt with the reality of what Jake had done to me, how he had used me.

After encouraging me to go ahead and kiss Jason, to give him a chance because he was a nice young man, Al left. So I was now out there alone with Jason. Jason looked into my eyes and laid his hand gently on my arm. There was such warmth and sincerity in those brown eyes, in that touch. My heart melted. He really did want me to give him a chance. It wasn't just some game he was playing. He really did like me. As if his continuing to try after two months wasn't enough of a clue. Duh, girl. When any other female he had found attractive didn't respond after a few days, he forgot about them. For some reason to him, I was different from any other girl he had met. Why did it take me so long to see it, believe it?

A few days later, I asked Jason to go for a walk with me as there was something I needed to do that he could help me with. We walked down to the lake and to the end of one of the piers. I took a ring off my finger. Just a cheap little ring, nothing special, that I had bought. The ring represented all my feelings for Jake, the love as well as the pain.

I spoke Jake's name out loud and said, "You had no right to treat me like you did. I loved you and you took advantage of my love and trust, my friendship. I deserve better." I think I even swore a little, releasing that anger and pain. Then I took the ring, said goodbye, and threw it as far as I could into the lake.

As Jason and I walked home I told him a little about what Jake had done to me, how he had hurt me. Jason was surprised by the cruelty and ignorance with which I had been treated. How, even with his own ignorance and inexperience, he would never hurt a girl like that. I joked around about any guy being with me it would be like having three girlfriends because of the Triplets. That is what the younger ones call the three oldest alters. Jason laughed.

Back up in Jason's apartment, he turned some music on and we danced. It was so much fun. I felt so good. A burden was thrown off my shoulders and a new possibility was right before me, shaking his hips. I left that night flying on a cloud. I so much wanted to kiss Jason goodnight. But I also wanted, needed to take things slow. I wasn't hoping for much, expecting too much, just a friend, someone to hang with and have fun with. I never expected there to be so much more between us. Neither, I think, did he.

It was when I invited Jason over for pizza and a movie that we had our first kiss. I was so nervous. I was afraid that I wouldn't feel anything. I was afraid I would be so terrible at it. We sat on chairs in my kitchen facing each other. He leaned in and pressed his lips to mine. Oh my! I sure did feel something and it was very mutual. Not mind blowing since we were both so nervous and the kiss tentative, but it was warm and gentle and very nice. I didn't even mind the tinge of cigarette smoke on his breathe. Surprising since I am allergic and never liked cigarette smoke.

Well, let's just say I overcooked the pizza a little. I was a bit distracted while it was in the oven. For the second kiss and the third, well took my breathe away. It was still edible though, the pizza. As we cuddled on the couch I asked him questions. What was his favorite color? Stuff like that, to get to know more about him. When I asked him what his favorite sweet was, he replied that I was. What better answer could he give, huh?

I told him it would be a good idea if we took things slow. See what develops as we hang out and get to know each other. He liked that idea. There was no need to rush into anything. Being new ground for me, I wasn't sure what I was doing. I didn't want to make any mistakes. I didn't want to "fall" too quickly, get swept away. I still had a lot of me work to do and that takes time and energy. I did not want to grow to depend on him too much or burden him with my past and all I go through. I needed to find out who I was, depend on me for my self-worth, and take care of myself. Even as I enjoyed and explored this relationship and the new ground I was treading.

We started hanging out a lot, Jason and I. He'd come over after work all eager to tell me about his day and to see me. We'd talk and cuddle and make out. There was a lot of chemistry between us as well as a growing respect.

We talked about things we didn't talk to anyone else about, comfortable to share some of the secrets of our pasts, to trust each other with them. I did not tell him too much about mine. I was having a hard time accepting it and even the little I told him was hard for him to hear.

Jason asked about the DID. Why was it they had to have separate names and ages? Why I wasn't just one name and age? I told him, "By these parts having a name of their own and an age, they can then reveal their secrets and begin to heal. It is not by choice I do this, but a necessity to survive what other people had done to me, the abuses I experienced."

Jason showed me over and over the man he really was and wanted to be. Although he had made mistakes that he was having a hard time forgiving himself for and suffered from Depression as well as Schizophrenia. He kept telling me before we hooked up, that opposites attract. Turns out, we have a lot more in common than he thought. The biggest opposite was that he was a smoker and I am allergic to cigarette smoke. Some alters more so than others. Knowing that, he was always sensitive and careful when he smoked around me.

I was so scared the first time we made love. Afraid he wouldn't like what I looked like. Afraid that I wouldn't be able to respond to him, even with all the chemistry we had between us. Afraid that it would hurt again, I would be hurt again. Afraid that he wouldn't like me anymore afterwards. Afraid that I wouldn't please him.

We had been making out on my couch, which was small. I was the one who suggested we move to my bedroom, where we would be more comfortable. He asked me if I would like to have sex. I could have said no and he would have respected that. But I didn't want to say no. I wanted to be with him, even though we hadn't been dating all that long. I was tired of playing by everyone else's rules. This was my life and I was going to do what I wanted to, no matter what other people thought. And if he didn't really like me, better to know now then later after I really fell for him.

We were both a little shy as we started taking our clothes off. But as we kissed and touched each other that shyness was replaced by the growing desire between us. Jason treated me with such gentleness and took his time. When he tried to enter me and my body wasn't ready, wouldn't open up to him, I began to cry. He didn't force it. He said it was okay and just held me.

When on another day as we made love and he was finally able to enter me, it did hurt a little. He held me close and gently moved against me, kissing me. Though, it wasn't until we had made love three or four times together that I was relaxed enough for us both to really enjoy it. Now how many males do you know who would be that patient and kind? Isn't that proof that there was something very special between us? Something you don't find every day? That he is an awesome guy?

Even after making love, we kept things slow between us. It wasn't until the Fourth of July when he called me his girlfriend for the first time. Then he backed it up a bit, saying I was his number one girl, his friend with benefits. Afraid I think to take that step with me. That was okay with me. We had only been seeing each other for a little over a month by then. I was scared too. I also knew that there were other girls he was interested in dating. Though I was the only one he was intimate with.

That was one thing we both made clear to each other when we started having sex. I am not the kind of girl that sleeps around. He assured me he wasn't that kind of guy either. Sex was something special he shared just with me. It was a matter of trust between us, a promise that we made to one another.

It might have been too soon in our relationship for sex. Yet there was some need within us both, for that tenderness, that comfort, that passion. It wasn't all we did together. It was but one aspect of our relationship.

I doubt few would understand. Sounds crazy doesn't it? Just starting to date each other and already being in a sexual relationship. He dating at times some other girl. I was free to date others too. I wonder if he even thought it out that far. After all, if it is okay for him and no big deal, then it should be okay for me, shouldn't it? I didn't, though, date anyone else. I didn't want to. But still if I had met someone I would have liked to hang out with watching a movie or go out to dinner with, I could have.

Neither of us was sure what we wanted or where this between us would go. I mean is that so wrong, to be best of friends with a special benefit? After all, both of us had been hurt and used and were unsure of many things. It might not be ideal in principle, but at that point in our relationship and in our individual healing with our specific illnesses, it worked for us. *(We were so ignorant of so many things weren't we?)*

As the months passed though, these other females seemed to me to be more of a distraction than anything else, since they only lasted a few days. It took me some time to understand why. Months in fact, not until after he had been in the hospital. The truth was that Jason was a multiple. He had three distinct parts to him at that time.

My therapist, Lynn explained to me that we all, everyone has different parts, or aspects to their personalities. They have different behaviors and masks that they wear in different situations around different people. Everyone has a little child inside them no matter how old they get.

114

Everyone has different roles they play as they progress through life. Being multiple is an extreme form of what is normal caused by extreme circumstances, severe abuse and traumas. Those experiences and its stresses cause a person to separate so fully in order to survive as to become separate identities.

The main part of Jason, that was my sweetheart. The open, friendly, and sociable side of him, who was not afraid to hold my hand, kiss me in public, and tell people that I was his girlfriend. Who could not get enough of me, was very much in love with me. Who would go to work and think of me even though surrounded by much prettier, thinner females.

One could not forgive himself for his past mistakes, but had to punish himself, and felt not good enough because of those mistakes. Eventually he came to feel like I was his friend. Maybe I was his only friend and the only person who truly understood and accepted him as he was.

Another part of him was full of anger and self-hate and had trust issues. He felt like it was him against the world and he was unloved and would never fit in anywhere, never be "normal". It was this side of him who would run off after some pretty girl he saw. He wanted the attention, to be liked, to be accepted. He was confused by why doing this left him feeling empty and lost and less accepted, less normal, used.

It did not help that he was being encouraged in this behavior, even after he and I had been together for some time. Not just by the media, movies, music, but by the males around him, friends and those he looked up to as role models. It didn't matter to them that he already had a girl. They told him, (and me both), that it was okay to run after any slight attraction and take full advantage, to sleep around as much as you could. It wasn't like we were married after all. Like it was no big deal. Like I didn't mean anything. Like relationships don't matter. Like respect is a joke.

Both Jason and I had seen first hand what living like that does to people and families and to relationships. It isn't healthy and can be very dangerous, both physically and emotionally. We both had been teased and had our sexual identities questioned, because we did not sleep around. Like there was, had to be something wrong with us. And really, if you can't respect a dating relationship how ever will you respect a marriage?

Truth was those that called us names and encouraged this kind of behavior, talked that kind of talk, were not happy themselves living like that. They were living lives of denial. Going from person to person, not letting anyone know them to protect themselves from being hurt again. Or they really felt so badly about themselves they believed no one could love them. Or they had an incapacity to connect to another human being on an emotional level and sex was one tool they used to manipulate and play games with people. Or that was all it was, just talk and they did not in truth act on it.

After spending just a little while with some girl, Jason would realize that he didn't really like them at all and stop seeing them. They were a fantasy, an illusion, a fleeting attraction to physical attributes, their shallow beauty, but not the person. After running like this after some other girl, he would be filled with guilt. He would tell me about it, though I always knew. There were clues after all. He hated hurting me and could not understand why he acted like this.

Usually these distractions followed some closeness he and I had shared. Perhaps that was how he reacted and dealt with his fear that I would leave him. A way to protect himself from a bigger hurt by suffering these little ones. Many of these females just used him and weren't really interested in him either. He was afraid to love me, to really trust me.

Other times this behavior happened when the depression or one of the negative symptoms of his Schizophrenia were acting up. There were times he felt disconnected to everyone, including me. Times when he felt like he had no friend in the world. Times when he would 'numb out" and not feel anything or feel empty inside. Times when he felt he was a horrible person for the mistakes he had made in the past and so acted out in some way to confirm it, to prove it.

Only one part of him was Schizophrenic. The positive symptoms of this illness, like delusions and hallucinations, were kept under control with medication so that Jason was able to hold down a job quite well. In fact, that summer he was working two jobs. So we really didn't have much time to spend together. I studied books and movies and programs on Schizophrenia to understand him better and know how to deal with this illness. Gail also being a Schizophrenic helped me a lot to understand the day to day aspects of the illness. How to handle the different ways it manifested itself in behaviors and attitudes and mood changes.

As the summer started dying down in August, I noticed something was happening in Jason. He wasn't sleeping. He quit one of his jobs hoping this would ease the stress he was under. It helped for a little while. He often came over late at night all jumpy, not being able to relax. We would play video games or watch a movie cuddling on the couch. Just by holding me, I would feel his breathing start to slow and his body relaxed. Sometimes I would rub out his shoulders or his back, which were often tight as a drum.

The Schizophrenic symptoms started to worsen. He would suddenly make some statement out of the blue, as if I had said something and he was responding to it, though I had said nothing. He would stare as if he were some place else in his mind. He would start rambling on and on about something, continually repeating the same things again and again and not able to concentrate on what anyone else said. The bouts of anger and depression grew worse also. I became very concerned about him.

Turns out he had stopped taking his medication. His mother had commented to him that he was on too many medications and so he stopped talking all of them. He confessed this to me one day while we were sitting in his apartment. He realized that he did indeed need the medication, at least the one to control the Schizophrenia. I agreed and encouraged him to start taking them again. He even signed a paper with the county psychiatric nurse. This paper gave me permission to give him his medication and to communicate with the staff about his condition. For him to do that meant that he trusted me.

He was no longer working. One of the jobs he had that summer and been trying to hold onto was seasonal and the season would soon end. He had recently bought a car and was trying to get his driver's license so that it would be easier for him to find another job.

Jason had a reaction to the first medication he was put on. It was one you dissolved on the tongue and it made his tongue numb. He even tried a drop of hot sauce to see if he could feel it. He felt that. Anyways, because of the reaction he was having they changed it. He had even a worse reaction to that one. His tongue swelled up and his jaw started twitching. It really scared him. He called up to social services and they called 911. I helped him talk to the First Responders, answer their questions and give to them all the medications of his that I had. I stood right behind Jason, my hand on his shoulder as they examined him in a chair.

Lynn was there, being head of the county's psychiatric department. She was the one who called me and told me what was going on. I don't know why Jason didn't come tell me first what was happening. Perhaps, he didn't want to worry me or thought he could handle it all himself.

I called Jason's dad and made sure he knew which hospital they were taking Jason for treatment. Jason's dad was really the only member of his family who was trying to help Jason at this time. He was really making an effort to listen to his son. He also knew that I was a big part of his son's life and really cared about him.

I held it together very well. Until I saw them put Jason up onto the gurney and wheel him out of the building. Then I lost it. I sat in a chair and cried and cried. I knew he was going to be okay. But to see someone you love wheeled out on a gurney like that and be driven off in an ambulance is a very scary and emotional sight.

The third medication they tried worked with no reactions, thank God. So the Schizophrenic symptoms were under control again. The rest of him though went way out of control. He grew very angry and his anger started scaring people. Just the tone in his voice or his words scared them, for some of them had been battered wives and I think his behavior was triggering them. They didn't want me anywhere near him, afraid for me, that he would start abusing me. But though he projected his anger towards me a couple of times, he never became abusive. Jason did not even realize he was acting like that. He had no idea why people were afraid of him.

What I didn't understand was that there was another Schizophrenic in the building who at times got angry and said things, who would become violent in his apartment and break things. They weren't afraid of him and understood it was due to his illness and he would soon calm down. But they couldn't or wouldn't understand Jason. That wasn't fair. After all Jason hadn't displayed any behavior like that in all the prior months he had lived there.

I was not afraid of him or his anger. I knew what it was like to be abused. For a while after moving to Green Lake, I even attended a support group for domestic abuse. I learned a lot. It was there that I realized that I had been abused by Jake and his family. They may have been subtle abuses, but those hurt and do damage too, even greater damage than a punch or kick does. I took the steps I needed to protect myself while still being there for Jason and to not allow or give opportunity for his projecting to become abusive.

I talked with Jason about it. He told me he wanted me to know how much pain he was in, wanted me to feel it. When I explained to him that I already knew, already felt his pain, the projecting stopped. His intent was never to have power or control over me, to blame me for his problems, or belittle me, which is the intent of abusers. He just wanted me to know how badly he felt. Though people were telling me to leave him and calling me stupid or worse, I was not going to desert him. I understood what was happening to him because I had been there myself. Yeah it was tough, very tough. But I loved him and he needed me, it would have been wrong to abandon him. We both had been abandoned enough.

Jason grew very depressed and talked of suicide. His fish died and I saw him bury it in the little garden in the backyard. I do not think he killed the creature. He told me, he yelled and swore at the fish, taking out his anger in that way at it. When the fish died, he blamed himself. Someone told me that he had killed his fish and chopped it into pieces, which of course frightened me. After talking to Jason and asking him what had happened though, I knew that was not true at all. I mean how could you bury something that was chopped into little pieces? It wasn't that big a fish.

One day he went over to his dad's house and got his hunting rifle and some shells. Another one of the tenants,

120

Lilith*, who had only recently moved in the beginning of September, rode with him, since he didn't have his license yet. She had her license and often took him out practicing. Though she had seen him pick up the gun, she did not tell anyone. She also happened to have been the one who had lied to me about him killing his fish and chopping it up. *(Something not quite right, huh?)*

I happened to see Jason bring the gun, which was inside a soft case, into the building and let Fred know about it. Fred called the police and was instructed to take the gun out of Jason's apartment and call Jason's dad to come pick it up. His dad had no idea that Jason has come to the house to get it. He had been at work at the time.

Clearly, Jason was in serious trouble. I think it was the very next day after the gun was removed from his apartment, the police came and took Jason away in handcuffs (I really hate that policy) to a psychiatric hospital in Madison. It was hard watching them take him away like that. But I knew that he needed help and that this was the only way.

I found the phone number and address of the hospital. I tried to call a few times but he refused to talk to anyone. I could understand him being angry. I remembered how angry I was when I was taken to the hospital. I wrote him two letters a week while he was there. He was there for three weeks. I took care of his plants and even cleaned up his apartment and washed his bedding, so it would be clean when he came home.

It was while cleaning that I found the box of shells for the rifle. I realized at that moment, looking at the red box, I had saved Jason's life. I knew he had the gun. I had no idea he already had the shells and was planning on shooting himself that very night. If I had not seen him come in with that rifle….If I had not known what it was he was carrying in….he would not be here today. Oh my! Can you imagine how that feels? Even now it bring tears to my eyes and twists my heart.

When he was gone about two weeks, Jason called me. He asked me to take care of his plants, which I told him I was already doing. I also told him that I had cleaned up his apartment. He really appreciated that. He told me he had received my letters, but hadn't read many of them yet. He stored them in his Bible for safe keeping. He knew I had tried to call him a few days after he had gotten there to the hospital, but he had slept for a couple of days straight and was sleeping when I called. It was good to hear his voice and know that he was doing much better.

At a halfway house he stayed at for a couple of days before coming home, he sent me a letter. Enclosed in the envelope with it was a white feather. The first love letter I ever received from him or anyone really. Here is what it said:

"*Rose,*

I'm just trying to make ends. I'll be ok now and forever. I got you and my Dad. I heard you cleaned. Thank you. I loved that you mailed me. I got a great new view on life. I miss being home but not too much. I didn't write you sooner because I didn't feel so good. Love you.

    Jason"

I couldn't wait for him to get home. I had been keeping busy helping to decorate the lobby and community room and planning a Halloween Party. The tenant association was no longer meeting. It usually planned all that kind of thing. I sure missed Jason, though. I knew he would be out of sorts for a while and would need time to get adjusted. I remember I was a tired mess when I came home from the hospital. I was willing to take it nice and slow. I just wanted him to be home, to see him, to hold him in my arms.

CHAPTER NINE

The day Jason came home from the hospital he surprised me. I was not expecting him for a few more days to a week. I hadn't been feeling well and so was up in my apartment. A friend of mine saw him come into the building and told him to go right up and see me. When I opened the door and saw him standing there...WOW!!! We held each other tight. It was so good to have him home again.

After making love, (well it was a long, very long three weeks and we missed each other badly), he invited me over to his apartment and we hung out together the rest of the afternoon. He told me that in the hospital they discovered three sides to him and about each part, including their names. We talked about a bunch of things. He asked me if I would consider marrying him in the future sometime, when we were both ready that is. I told him yeah, if we were still together and were ready, I would consider it.

Jason got angry at me a few minutes later. He had asked me to go to his mother's house with him for Thanksgiving dinner. I told him I couldn't. I had a dinner here for those in the building who didn't have any place to go. He didn't even give me a chance to explain or to maybe try and do both. To get back at me he asked this girl he had met at the hospital to go with him on Thanksgiving and be his girlfriend. He even gave me the phone and had us talk to each other. He was acting out, like a little kid would who was upset or scared or disappointed. He had switched to another alter.

I knew that he would still be out of sorts and unstable when he came home and that is was possible he would suddenly get mad at me over something little, say things he didn't mean. He was still a little bit angry at me when Lilith came over. She was supposed to be my friend, yet she acted like I had no right to be there in Jason's apartment and was very angry at me. Her eyes were black, literally black. I mean she knew Jason and I were together. What was her problem? It made me feel very uncomfortable. When while joking around with me Jason's knuckles hit mine a little too hard, sending pain shooting up my arm, I had to leave. He needed a chance to cool down. Lilith being there seemed to make the anger shoot up in him again.

The next day, I was in the community room working on a puzzle, visiting with neighbors, when Lilith and Jason came into the room. Jason asked me if I liked the flower he had left on my door. I said, "Thank you. I didn't know that it was from you." I mean a couple of times Lilith had given me a flower for me being a friend to her and so had Gail.

Jason's face grew all dark and he said, "How many of your other boyfriends leave you flowers?" He was serious. He really thought I had other boyfriends. I told him, "You are my only boyfriend. There has never been any other."

He gave me a look like he didn't believe me and left the room with Lilith to go get drunk with her. She was caring a pack of beer and had said that she and Jason were going to go drink it. She was daring anyone to say anything, daring me more than anyone else in the room. Not a good thing for someone recently out of the hospital and still unstable to do, drink. Lilith should have known better. Just another clue to the truth of the kind of person she was.

I know there were rumors around the building, mainly started by this bitter old woman with too much time on her hands, that I had all these guys on a string. The only other guys in my life were my brother Dante and Todd who was strictly a friend. Todd was in the Navy and homesick and I was writing to him to help him. I mean he had stuck by me, stayed my friend when I lost everyone else around me. It was the least I could do for him, right. I joked around a little bit with Fred, but he was like my uncle.

Once in a while I talked to some male on-line about whatever, just as you might strike up a conversation with someone at the store or on the street. What is wrong with that? I talked to females that way too. It didn't make them boyfriends or potential boyfriends. But in the idle mind of a bitter woman who lives to play games with people, it was fuel for her private soap opera. Someone, maybe even several people were making sure to whisper these rumors into Jason's ear, trying to convince him they were true. As if his mind wasn't a confused jumbled mess already.

The lies and rumors played on his own fears and his self-doubts. He was afraid to believe me, to trust me, to really open his heart to me. He was afraid that once I got to know him, that once he loved me, I would abandon him and not love him anymore. I understand those fears as I have them myself. All these relationship things being new to me, I was making mistakes too.

Late the next night, Lilith came knocking on my door. She was all in tears. I let her in, invited her to sit down, and talked to her. She showed me her arms, which were full of scratches and shallow cuts. I went and got some hydrogen peroxide and cotton balls to clean them while I listened to her. The cuts were not fresh, but at least a day old and had already started healing. She talked about her boyfriend, who was out west.

(Jason told me, when we were talking again, that the night of the drinking Lilith got mad at him about something. She broke one of his disposable razors, took the blade, and started cutting up her arm right in front of him. That really

freaked him out and he didn't know what to do. Those were the scratch marks she showed me the following night.)

Then Lilith dropped a bomb on me. She told me she had had sex with Jason. Oh, she said she didn't mean to, that it just happened. She said over and over that she was sorry and didn't want to loose my friendship. I didn't believe her. Something like that doesn't just happen. There was something about her behavior that wasn't right, didn't feel right to me. I had the feeling she wasn't sorry at all. Then there was the fact that around her neck she was wearing Jason's necklace, one he wore all the time. I had been his girl for how long and here she was wearing it. Yeah, okay something definitely was rotten in Denmark.

She wasn't really my friend and didn't care if she lost my friendship. If I were really her friend and she valued that, then she would never have had sex with him. She would have respected my relationship with Jason. Not taken advantage of him when he was in a vulnerable state.

I was in shock as you can imagine. I didn't process through it all till later. It sunk in when I realized she wasn't my friend and never had been. I remembered the little looks of jealousy and anger when she saw me and Jason together, saw the tenderness and love between us. I noticed that she didn't spend much time with me and Jason together, but usually it was with us separately. Like she had to be the center of our attention. Like she was already trying to separate the two of us. Something just wasn't right.

I got angry, very angry. I refused to talk to either one of them. I never even confronted Jason about it, asked him if it had happened. I should have. But he had been drinking, with his medications he wouldn't have remembered what happened anyways. A couple of days later, I was talking to a woman who used to live in the building and still cleaned for people here. She told me that Lilith had told her Jason and I had broke up a long time ago.

I told her, no. I only just broke it off with him for

having sex with Lilith. She was surprised to hear it. Lilith had been telling lies about Jason and me for some time it seems. Some friend. No wonder she was so mad I was at Jason's when he came home from the hospital. She had been telling everyone that he and I had broken up.

When my phone bill came, there were extra charges added to it. Things I had not given permission for. An extra service had been added by Lilith. I found that out when I called the phone company asking them about it, wanting it removed. There was also several long distance calls. Lilith had been coming into my apartment and using my phone without my permission while I was downstairs. I was stupid and trusting and had left my door unlocked and she knew that. A mistake I never repeated again, I can assure you.

That is all Lilith wanted from me, my phone and some place to run to so she didn't have to sit alone in her apartment. I was someone to listen to her and feel sorry for her. I was used, just plain used, by someone who pretended to be my friend, but really wasn't. My kind nature taken advantage of by a person with no heart, no conscious.

People understood why I was mad at Jason, but not why I was mad at Lilith. Um...were they a few cards short of a deck or something? I had more reason to be angry with Lilith. She took advantage of Jason totally. He had just gotten out of the psychiatric hospital from a complete breakdown for crying out loud. Anyone who has ever had a breakdown, even a mild one, knows that it takes time for everything to get "normal" again. You are a bunch of volatile emotions and oversensitive, easily confused, just a mess.

Jason was being chased by three women after coming home from the hospital: Lilith, that girl he had met at the hospital, and the college age daughter of a woman who was staying in Fred's apartment on weekends. Fred went home to his family on the weekends. His apartment, being the manager's apartment was the only one with two bedrooms and a separate dining room off the kitchen. This woman was a friend of his and needed a place to stay. Jason was blamed for something that had happened in Fred's apartment one weekend, which totally pissed Fred off. When Fred found out about me breaking up with Jason he was very glad.

Jason wasn't chasing them, these females. They were chasing him. They were calling him, going to his apartment looking for him, following him around. He liked the attention. I mean, come on, what male wouldn't, especially one who wasn't used to it? All three knew that he had been with me and didn't care. I mean they were chasing him before he and I even broke up.

One had just chased and used him that previous summer. She had approached him and a friend of his and told them all the things she would do for them, to them, if you know what I mean. Of course, it was all just talk. She had no intention of doing anything. She was just playing them for her own amusement. Too many females act like that. It makes it bad for us nice girls who wouldn't even dream of treating anyone like that. Yet guys fall for it and hurt us when they do. Yet who do they turn to when they get hurt? Yeah, us. Then they have the audacity to call us stupid and foolish for trusting or going off with a "bad" guy. Please.

For a week, I was very angry. I called Jason names, really acted out. I think part of it was due to all the stress from his breakdown and people not understanding and laying on me hard to abandon him. It was not an easy thing to go through, emotionally. To watch someone you love go through that and not know what to do, how to help, to almost lose them to the deep darkness of depression. With everything else on top of that... I lost it in anger for a while. I could have broken down myself. It is a wonder that I didn't.

During that week, Lilith pretended to be Jason's girlfriend. She acted like it was no big deal. Fred thought that girl friends shouldn't fight over some guy. No guy is worth it. Maybe most guys aren't, or maybe Fred just didn't feel like he is worth it. However, friends don't do that to each other. Not if they really are friends. If I didn't believe Lilith wasn't sorry about having sex with Jason before, I certainly didn't believe her now.

Wasn't it obvious this was her plan all along? Maybe even from the very first day she met him soon after moving in? She and I were in the community room talking and working on a puzzle. I went down to the bathrooms and when I came back, Jason was sitting there at the table talking to her. The second I came into the room his attention was focused on me. It was obvious how he felt about me, that he wasn't interested in her like that. I guess it was something she wasn't used to and she didn't like it.

Well, Lilith's pretense lasted only two days. Jason caught her cheating on him with some other guy and broke it off. He met some other girl and started dating her. Lilith pulled her shit again. She "seduced" him to break them up. Then she got Jason and her latest "boyfriend" (who was only 18) plastered. While Jason was passed out on his floor, Lilith took his car keys and her and this other guy went for a joyride. They ended up sending the car into a ditch and doing $400.00 worth of damage to the under-carriage plus damage to the tires from doughnuts this kid had been doing.

Not one bit of responsibility did Lilith take for it. She only said that Jason had given her permission to take his car and that other guy, who didn't even have a license and she was well aware of that fact, was driving. Umm… how could Jason give permission when he was passed out on the floor huh? Why would he give anyone who was drunk, permission to drive his car in the first place? Did he give her permission on some other day and she felt this was a general permission to take his car whenever she wanted to? Used that as her "excuse"?

But you know, people backed her up and not Jason. I couldn't believe it. Here this 31-year-old woman, a mother of two children, not real small children either but older children from 10 to teenage, working on getting a divorce, was providing alcohol to under-agers. "Dating" one guy after another who was typically from 18 to 20, using them and people thought that was okay. She wasn't wrong or at fault for anything. They thought it was wrong for me to have ever been with Jason. Even though he was the only boyfriend I had ever had and I never used or manipulated him in any way. I treated him with respect and love and stuck by him when everyone else was running away and wanted nothing to do with him. Crazy! Pure insanity. There's no other way to describe it. Insanity!

Jason came up to me one morning when I was on my way to a chiropractor appointment. He asked me," Did you break up with me out of guilt for me being in the hospital? Your letter said that you felt sorry for it."

What!!! I told him, "No. I didn't break up with you when you were in the hospital. I know what I wrote in all my letters. I said I understood your anger for being in the hospital, but I never felt guilty for it." I mean I had saved his life. What was there for me to feel guilty about? I had done the right thing.

Jason looked confused. I would be too. He offered to walk me to my appointment and I let him. I was over being angry. It wasn't his fault all that had happened. He was just as much a victim as I was, just as hurt. It was nice being able to talk to him again.

I think what "woke him up" was something that happened in the community room one day. A new male tenant had been making me very uncomfortable staring at me. You know that kind of stare I mean, as if I was just

130

female parts and not a person. Jason suggested to him that he try "asking" me out.

I worked on puzzles a lot for a while. It was something to do and a way for me to socialize. While I sat there, people would come in for a few minutes and chat or help with the puzzle. When I was stressed or anxious, I would bring my music and headphones down. It really helped me to relax and work through things.

Jason waited out in the hallway, while this man entered the community room to talk to me. I knew Jason was out there, listening. I told the man, "No. I am not interested. I have only ever had the one boyfriend. I do not want another one. I am done."

While this man and I talked, and Jason listened, he heard a tone in my voice when I said Jason's name. "You still love him don't you?" He asked me.

"Yes. I do." I replied.

That was when this man realized he didn't stand a chance with me. I also told him that I didn't appreciate the way he was looking at me. It made me very uncomfortable when he stared at me like that. I am not that kind of girl. This surprised him, I think. From then on, he treated me with more respect.

Thanksgiving Day, Jason came and ate a little with me and the others who were down in the community room. I really appreciated that, even though he was to meet his family at a church a little later. He took a picture of me. I look like a scared girl in that picture and didn't know what to do with my arms. I looked pretty, even if scared and gave Jason a copy of it. I took a few pictures of him, showing him in different moods, playful and more serious. His presence there helped me get through it, even if he could only stay for a while and had to leave.

I try to buy a disposable camera to take pictures of functions like this. Not just for my Memory Book, but also for the little photo album that Jean* and I had put together for the building. I started the Memory Book in Berlin around Jake's 18th birthday. It was a good way to record memories and moments and accomplishments. With that and my journals I can't really forget anything, even those things I might want to.

Jean was this sweet little old lady with a green thumb and a cat, which resembled a mini lion. She had come to the first Thanksgiving dinner we had had back when I moved in. Like me, she was trapped inside a shell. Over the months as I got to know her and helped her with the decorations, she began to emerge a beautiful butterfly. The littles now call her Granny. Okay, all of us do really. She doesn't have any grandchildren of her own and thinks of both Jason and I as her grandkids. We have become close and understand each other well.

That Sunday Jason came into the community room. The only lights on were these little spot lights in the ceiling over the table where the puzzle was. He asked me for a hug. It was so good to be in his arms again. He started to kiss me and held me so close to him. We made up that day, made up very well, four times well in fact.

He asked me to go with him over to his mother's. They were having their Thanksgiving dinner. He said he needed me to be there with him and made up this secret signal for when he felt like he had to leave. I was nervous about it, having never met her before. I felt funny since we had just got back together and hadn't even been dating all that long. Well, not long enough for the meet the parents kind of thing. But maybe five months is long enough. I don't know. I was scared about what she would think of me, how she would react to me. But Jason needed me and so I agreed to go with him.

She didn't appreciate him bringing me and let him know it the next time she talked to him. She told him I was "nice", but "too old" for him. She knew nothing about me, nothing, and didn't try to. She had made her judgment just by how I looked. Just because I have an air of maturity instead of the shallow flightiness of most females. Whatever. But while I was there, they were all friendly enough.

We stayed a while, visiting, and ate dinner with them. When he was done eating Jason went outside for a cigarette. He was ready to go home. He had given me the secret signal a little earlier. He was shaky and growing upset. I talked to him and said okay we can go. We just had to go inside and tell them all goodbye first.

On the drive home, he played a guy band and sang me love songs while holding my hand. He told me he loved me and we were going to try to stay together until at least Valentine's Day. Sounded like a good goal to me.

CHAPTER TEN

The year 2005 came to an end. What a year it had been! The next year started full of promise.

Jason and I were still together come Valentine's day. He surprised me by bringing me a red rose. I told him I was going to save it. He told me don't worry. There will be more where that came from. Of course I saved it anyways. I mean it was my first rose after all from my first Valentine.

We had one shaky part before then. He had been distracted by some girl and ended up cheating on me with her. He felt really bad, torn with guilt over it. He was honest with me about it, telling me what had happened and how he felt.

He was afraid that I wanted more from him and from our relationship than what he was ready for. That I should be with someone who was ready to marry me, that I should be married and having children. That though he loved me, he found himself attracted to other females and wondering what it would be like to date them. He felt terrible right after having sex with this other girl. Felt so torn up from hurting me. He hating hurting me and didn't want to hurt me any more. He figured it would be better if we just were friends. That he loved me more as a friend and didn't feel that forever after kind of love with me.

I told him that I was not ready for marriage or children either, far from ready. I had too much healing I needed to do first. I was just taking our relationship step by step, day by day. I told him okay, we would try to be just friends. All I was expecting from our relationship was just to take it as it was, to enjoy our time together for however long it lasted. We were best of friends as well as lovers. It was just a matter of taking the sex out of it, right.

For a week or two we did try to be just friends as he dated this other girl. I curbed my behavior with him. No more flirting, no more kisses, only a quick friend hug. We hung out together, talked, played games, watched movies, listened to music. It was nice though it wasn't easy. All those things I was used to, loved having the freedom to do, to feel, I couldn't any more. Actually, it was quite frustrating to tell the truth.

One day while we were playing a board game that he had bought, we were talking about something and I said, "Well, it isn't like I have a boyfriend anyways." I was angry and frustrated from having to hold myself back so much. I had thought it would get easier. It hadn't. Not to mention I had been depressed and felt bad about how I looked, that whole poor self-image thing.

Jason said, "Yes you do. I am your boyfriend."

I looked at him. There was a look of hurt in his eyes. I was confused. I told him what he had said to me that night after being with that other girl. That I had curbed my behavior, backed up a little and were just friends with him like he had said he wanted, while he dated her.

Jason told me that I didn't need to change my behavior with him. That he had thought by my backing up from him like I did that I didn't like him anymore, didn't want to be with him anymore, and didn't love him anymore. He didn't remember saying those things to me that night, didn't remember us deciding to be just friends.

What else doesn't he remember? It was like one hand didn't know what the other was doing, saying, feeling. It was very confusing. I understood then how confusing I was to him, with all my alters and changes in how I reacted to him, in how I felt about him. Being a multiple is not easy, not at all, nor is being in a relationship with one.

Jason told me that he didn't want to be with anyone else but me. He was tired of these other girls just using him. He was tired of thinking some girl was pretty and nice, wanting to be with her, to see what happens, if she is the "one". Then after spending a little time with her finding that they had nothing in common, no connection, and that he didn't really like her after all. It left him feeling terrible about himself. But being with me he felt good. I understood him. I listened. I loved and accepted him just as he was. I was the drug that calmed him, comforted him. He loved me.

It was a good time for us as a couple. Others in the building though didn't see it that way. That one bitter old woman with too much time on her hands started spreading rumors and making comments every time she saw us together. Told Jason how he was doing so much better away from those two females, meaning me and Lilith, even though she knew full well me and him were still together. She called me Jason's "mommy". That I had to be with him wherever he went, was controlling him, that kind of stuff. None of it true of course. But people listened and didn't think it through for themselves.

Even Gail would sometimes throw at me some of this shit being said. She should have known better, known me better than that. I don't know if it was from her Schizophrenia and just blurting out what she had been hearing or if it was her jealousy over what was between me and Jason, or some combination of both. But it hurt to have a friend, someone I trust, who should know me treat me like that. It hurt that friendship.

It hurt Jason as much as it did me, the things being said, and he curbed our public displays of affection because of it. We weren't all that affectionate in public anyways, once in a while holding hands. He gave me a kiss once right in the parking lot. Mostly that stuff was kept behind closed doors. It was our business anyways, right? So I wasn't even to touch his arm or call him by some endearment or anything when that woman was anywhere around. I understand him wanting to cut down on the "talk", but reacting that way also gave her power and it didn't make things better, just worse.

This bitter old woman wasn't the only one making comments. Some of the ladies in the Community Room at lunch time also "talking". Not just about me and Jason being together, how I wasn't good enough for him and had no right to be with him. No, they attacked me personally, my disorder, my arthritis. One woman made the statement that DID wasn't real. Only criminals fake DID in order to get away with something. That really angered me. Others said I was faking the arthritis for attention.

Umm I go to a chiropractor twice a month and it has been documented on x-rays the arthritis in my back and hips, as well as a curve in my spine and severe whiplash, so my neck is straight instead of curved like it should be. The DID and PTSD and Chronic Depression are also documented. But even if I had brought in all this evidence to show them, it wouldn't change a thing. They would still continue on believing and saying whatever suits them regardless of the truth.

Some of this I myself heard as I sat in the lounge reading. It made me very uncomfortable not just to be in the Community Room, but also in the lounge and I started spending more and more time upstairs, afraid to come down. The longer it went on the more afraid I became, even to just go down to get my mail, when I knew that they would be in that room.

Granny Jean was very upset by it all. She ate lunch in there nearly every day there was a meal. It wasn't just hearing them say all those terrible things about me. They would push her for information, information about my relationship with Jason, about anything regarding me. When she said anything, responded in any way, they pushed her for more. If she didn't say anything, they would get mad and shun her. She grew very uncomfortable eating there and had to start canceling meals.

Being on a special diet for an illness she has, there were certain things Granny Jean couldn't eat. The stress made her condition all the worse. She discovered through studying about her illness that there were more foods she needed to avoid. That was a good excuse to cancel even more meals and make them herself in her apartment or go to the little restaurant up the street.

Granny Jean couldn't believe how cruel they were being to me and to her. I couldn't believe it either. People who once accepted me as I was or I thought had now openly were attacking me and my character like it was no big deal. I am sure other people who heard all this going on were also upset by it. I wasn't the only target either of this "gossip" and slander, but I did seem to be their favorite.

It put a strain on my relationship with Jason, as I was afraid to leave my apartment more and more. I was afraid to do much of anything. Sometimes I would with no problem. We even drove up to Appleton once and hung out at a mall up there on a busy weekend night. I wasn't scared in any way that night. No one looked at us funny or made comments about him and me being together, holding hands as we looked at the displays.

In fact when we walked around town together we only got positive looks if anyone looked at all. A couple of times this elderly couple saw us and just smiled. They thought we were cute together. No, the only problems, bad reactions we got were from some here in the apartment building and his family. The ones who should know better than anyone how we treated each other, how good we were together, how I had stayed by him when he was having his breakdown.

Then that Easter of 2006 my brother, Dante was nearly killed, which sent me crashing. His one foster sister had been visiting him for a week and he was traveling with her to Phoenix to spend a week with her. They had arrived on Easter Sunday at the bus station. Dante saw a lady in distress and being the kind of guy he is, he went to help her. Seems some man had stolen her purse. While Dante talked to and tried calming the woman down, his sister went to go get security. The man who had snagged her purse was still there in the station close by. He went up to Dante and stabbed him in the abdomen with a knife.

One of Dante's friends sent me a message about Dante being in trouble. I had already felt that something was wrong and when I hadn't heard from him for several days I had become very worried. The following week Dante's foster sister told me the whole story. Dante was in a coma for almost a week. He spent many weeks in the hospital recovering. He has a permanent bone chip in his hip as a constant reminder of that day.

Dante and I had become so close, really like twins. To almost loose him, really floored me, like I had almost lost a piece of me. We knew just what to say to each other when we were having a rough time. He understood all the things I went through, since he went through them himself. Though separated by several states physically, we were connected in another way. Like real birth twins are. That was how we felt about each other. Real family.

Jason didn't understand. He was jealous of the amount of time I spent talking to Dante on the computer. The messages we sent back and forth. The cards and letters we sent in the mail. I could talk to Dante about anything and everything, especially about things I was feeling, my depressions, and my flashbacks. Jason talked all day at work and didn't want to talk when he got home. I didn't push it, but that lack of communication is what was causing some of our problems.

Honestly, I didn't really give Jason much of a chance. I poured it out to Dante and kept other things for Jason. One was my heart. The other was my soul. I had a hard time explaining to Jason why I was broken up inside my mind, that it wasn't just a game for attention. How could it be when I spent most of my time inside my apartment when I was going through something? No one knew what I really went through, because I didn't let them. It clearly wasn't a game for attention, as I was getting no attention from it, just the opposite.

I was afraid to let Jason know about my past, about those horrors. I was having a hard time dealing with them. I would say we or her but would not say I had this happen to me. I could not own my own reality, much less expect Jason to understand or believe it. I made excuses why I couldn't go out dancing or to play pool with him. He thought I didn't want to. Truth was I was afraid. But I didn't tell him that. I didn't give him a chance to understand, to be there for me, to help me. I kept part of me closed off to him.

I also did it, kept quiet to hide and escape for a little while from this reality I was dealing with. I just wanted to be warm and have fun and laugh and smile sometimes. To just forget for five minutes my horrible past and concentrate on the here and now. That is understandable isn't it?

As spring headed towards summer, the attacks on me were still going on. Jason knew about it and didn't understand why I let them get to me so bad. We started spending less time together. I was closed off, too afraid all the time. I wasn't in any therapy at this time. I hadn't been since the previous November. It was a lot to try to handle all on my own.

It was the perfect opportunity for those who were jealous of what Jason and I had together or who were just prejudiced against the mentally ill to strike. This girl, Abbey* Jason met at work. From the day she met him she started pushing him to be her boyfriend. He told her he wasn't interested in her in that way and just wanted to be friends, to hang out sometimes. But she wouldn't accept that.

Abbey was always calling Jason and following him here after work or having him go over to her parent's house. He didn't have any free time to himself, much less time to be with me, because she was always with him. Some of our friends asked Jason how I was in front of her, prompting Abbey to ask Jason who I was. He was honest with her. He told her I was the girl who lived down the hall and was in love with him. Abbey asked him how he felt about me. He told her he loved me too. Still she did not back off.

She started telling everyone that she was Jason's girlfriend. Of course those who did not "approve" of us being together in the first place backed her up. They were friendly with her and encouraged her. It is quite possible that a few of these individuals actually set up Jason and me. That is planned on Abbey going after Jason to separate us or just using her, helping her. There were just too many things that didn't add up. How they treated Abbey, like she was their good friend though they had all "just met". Abbey running into the Community Room during a cookout to give Lilith a huge hug and thank her. Stuff like that.

Jason knew I was being attacked, but I don't think he understood the severity of it, why I was so afraid. He laughed off some of the comments being made and said he had my back, not to worry about it. I tried. It was all too much, with being worried about my brother and my own inner stuff along with it.

On Mother's Day after visiting his mom Jason came to see me. He told me what Abbey was doing, the pressure she was putting on him to be her boyfriend. He kept telling her he wasn't interested, but she wouldn't listen. I told him I knew about her calling herself his girlfriend. He didn't seem to think it that big a deal. She was a girl and his friend that was how he saw it. He loved me and that was what mattered.

But that isn't how Abbey saw it, meant it. She kept up the pressure, these other people here in the apartment building and I don't know who else, helping. He should have stopped hanging with her, told her to back off. That was hard when he worked with her, and she just wouldn't listen.

Jason was confused and depressed one night. Abbey was there as she usually was. She kept asking him what's wrong and touching him. He just wanted to be left alone. So he went to lie down in his room. He told her she could stay or leave, whatever. She went into his room and got up on his bed next to him and started touching him, kissing him, saying she loved him, what's wrong, on and on, pressing him. She had been saying she loved him since she met him. How could she when she didn't even know him?

He should have had her leave. He should have told her to stop, to get off him. Maybe he did, tried to. But Abbey only hears what she wants to hear. She ended up forcing him to have sex with her. He may not see it that way, after all he is a guy. But he was in a compromised emotional state. He was in no condition to give consent and had told her over and over he wasn't interested. Isn't that a definition of sexual assault? Isn't that what Jake and Todd had done to me?

Jason came to talk to me the next day very upset. He told me what had happened. He was scared she would become pregnant even though he did not enter her. He was so confused and lost. He said, "I should be with her just in case she does get pregnant."

I told him, "You can't base a relationship on that. It won't work."

142

He said, "Maybe we should just be friends and that is all," meaning me and him.

"We have tried that already. It didn't work because there is more between us than just friendship. We love each other."

I urged him to take the time to think things through. He said he would. Then he asked me if I wanted to go swimming with him. I said okay and he left to get ready and give me time to get my suit on.

We drove to a parking lot near the beach, but he changed his mind and wanted to go back home. "Okay", I told him. Back in the parking lot of our apartment building we stood, silent. I told him to think about things and let me know what he decides.

"I have already decided." He said. "I am going to be with her."

I was devastated of course. He didn't take any time to think, not really. But he had decided so I had to react. I could have gotten angry and yelled and begged or something, but I didn't. I said, "If that is your decision then I will respect that. But do not treat me as something to fall back on if it doesn't work out. I won't be treated like that. It isn't fair to me." He agreed that wouldn't be fair.

Back in my apartment I collapsed. It wasn't fair. It wasn't right. Why was he giving in to her? Did he think by giving in that the attacks on me would stop and I wouldn't have to be so afraid anymore? What was he thinking? He was worried about her getting pregnant so had to be with her just in case. But what about all the times we had had sex and weren't always careful. Where was his concern about my getting pregnant? What about his loving me, me loving him? Didn't any of that matter?

CHAPTER ELEVEN

A lot of things happened in that year since we had met, Jason and I. Things I did not know till I read through my journals. Since it was more than one of us inside involved in this relationship, for both me and Jason I didn't, couldn't know all that happened between us. The memories of us inside are our own and we only share some things to reduce confusion.

Jason and I played that game of come here-go away so many of us play. He wanted me to like him, when I did it scared him. It was the same for me. We would get closer then back off and not see each other for days. What we were starting to feel scared us almost as much as our pasts. It was something neither one of us had felt before and we didn't know what to do. So we kept making all these mistakes.

We weren't ready for all that it would mean and lead to. We were trying to just take it one day at a time, to define our relationship as we needed it to be, what we were ready for. That is hard to do with no good role models and people starting to interfere more and more. Hard, with him having this image of me, seeing me as so much more mature and together than he was. Truth was I was just as confused and mixed up and unsure of everything as he was. Just as inexperienced and young.

There was definitely something special between us though and no matter how far we tried to run, how much we tried to hide from each other and what we were feeling, we would find ourselves together again. We kept running in this big circle just to return to one another's arms. Needing, wanting what lay in each other's eyes, in our souls, and finding no one else who made us feel so alive, so free to just be ourselves. We grew to be best friends as well as sweethearts, lovers.

I entered a poetry contest at the local library and won. That encouraged me to really seriously think about publishing a book of them. I had one I had written years back before I started breaking down. During my "nun years" as I called them. The poems dealt with faith issues when you are going through hardships.

I knew that no major publisher would pick it up since not as many people read anymore and they are pickier about what they will consider. Besides with my income I couldn't afford to make so many copies of the manuscript and mail it off to so many different publishers with no guarantee anyone would read it much less publish it.

Then one day Gail gives me this web address for a self-publishing firm. I was curious yet hesitant. I had checked out one before and the cost was too high for my budget. Turns out this one is free. That was perfect. The only cost would be the copies I bought and any promoting materials and services I wanted to buy.

I went ahead and did it. I got my first book published. I was so proud when I held it in my hands, seeing my name on the cover. Not that many months later I published a second one. This one of poems I had written as I was breaking down and dealing with so many things from panic attacks and depression to friendships and family, which I dedicated to Jason and my brother, Dante.

Jason accomplished much in that year we were together too. He bought a car, outright, no loan and got his diver's license. He started going back to school to get his GED. He was back working once things settled from his breakdown and was doing very well. He was starting to walk down his own healing journey, taking care of himself and his apartment.

We brought out he best in each other. Being together was like a drug that lessened our fears as well as bringing comfort and ease from our pains. We made each other happy. We walked around with smiles on our faces and a sparkle in our eyes. Of course our fears and self-doubts and our mistakes brought tears and anger and confusion too. Love is not all happiness and flowers. Relationships are not always easy and smooth flowing. But that is what makes it all the more real and refines it, makes it stronger. Every hardship we encountered helped us to appreciate each other more, appreciate what we had together.

When Jason started "dating" Abbie that summer of 2006, we were both miserable. It wasn't what either one of us wanted and yet he felt he had no choice. Under that much pressure from Abbie and others around him and me being attacked so badly, what else was he to do? He tried to get out of it, to get away from her, but she wouldn't listen. The pressure on him did not ease nor the attacks on me stop just because he had given in.

I spent a lot of time with Granny Jean and Gail. I went down to the beach. I actually got in the water again and started swimming. Something I hadn't been able to do in a long time. I had been afraid of water, especially lake water since I drowned once as a little girl. But I loved the water too, had since I was a baby. The memory I had recovered with my real family at the beach helped me fight my fear and enjoy the water again.

I was bold and bought a pink bikini. Of course I had to buy material to add to the top. They don't really make swimsuits for full figured females, least not with my figure, unless you custom make it and who has that kind of money? Not me for sure. It was Red's idea. She thought, why not? We were working hard to trim down and firm things up. It would remind Jay what a fool he was for giving in and being with someone else. Make him think and maybe be afraid of some other guy coming along and stealing me away.

I don't really play those games and don't think I should have to. More often than not that kind of thing backfires. I just wanted him to remember what he had. I guess too I figured I was free. He was with someone else letting her sleep in his bed. Why should I sit around my apartment all day, not having any fun, crying all the time? If I happened to meet anyone I wanted to hang with I could. Though that was all it would be, friendship.

Of course I didn't. I had fun swimming. I got a lot of looks. But guys I saw just reminded me of Jason. I continually compared them to him and they always fell short. I just wasn't interested. I was still too much in love with Jason and knew he still loved me and was utterly miserable with Abbie.

She was very jealous and possessive and abusive. He wasn't allowed to go anywhere or do anything unless it was okay with her. If he had the audacity to come see me, even just to talk and hang out as friends, he would get into trouble. See it didn't help my apartment was being watched, I was being watched, and every time we were around each other, Jason and I, someone would report it to Abbie. Or there would be more rumors and slanders against me, more teasing of him for being with me, to make him back away. We weren't even allowed to be neighborly much less friends.

During that year we were together and that summer he was with Abbie I was doing a lot of inner work. Dealing with all these things from my past I was remembering on top of the social abuses I was dealing with in the here and now. That is what all those rumors and slanders and gossip are, social abuse. Do what we want, be who we want you to be or be shunned and tore down. There were social abuses with my other periods of abuse. It is all part of the abuse wheel after all. Subtle, yet hurtful all the same, even more hurtful then a kick or punch.

I was learning to own my traumas. Not an easy thing to do. Being multiple I could say this happened to her, because it did. Even though this is one body and it happened to this body, different ones inside experienced and hold those memories. It was very hard to say, "I was raped." "I was beaten and left in a puddle of pain." But I started to and found it freeing. The very reason for the alters was to hold the memories so I could survive and live on the next day, go to school and pretend all is well so no one knew my secret.

I was afraid for people to know my secret. Afraid they would hate me. I was afraid to tell Jason these things and shared them more with my brother, because I was afraid Jason would hate me too, like Jake had. I really didn't want Jason to hate me. I needed his love and friendship. Thing is Jason already knew. We talked more when we first started dating, talked about stuff like this. But as we grew closer and cared about each other more and more we stopped talking and sharing these things as much. In the beginning if it scared one of us off it wasn't that big a deal. Falling in love with each other changed that. It was now a very big deal and we could not risk the other hating us as we often hated ourselves.

Jason would often be surprised that I didn't hate him, didn't yell at him or say he was an awful person when he shared some secret of his from his own past with me. I understood and accepted and loved him just as he was, mistakes and all, weaknesses and all. That was hard for him to deal with. Well I had the same struggle. We both kept wondering, okay when are things going to change? Waiting for that proverbial shoe to drop like it always had before. But it never did drop. It wasn't going to drop. With regards to other people around us who came in and out of our lives, yes. With regard to each other, no.

When Jason needed me I was there for him even though him being with Abbie and how she was treating him tore me up. I couldn't turn him away. I would get so angry and tell myself no more, enough, I can't take this. But then I would look at his face, into those chocolate brown eyes and the anger would melt away. I would just surrender to the love between us and that would be all that mattered in that moment. Our hearts and souls were forever connected no matter how many people tried to keep us apart.

Finally that September Jason was able to break away from her. He had struggled for so long to get away, to stop this. Hating himself all the more for what he was putting me through. He had been so angry all summer, isolated by her. He felt real good to be free again. I felt good too. Good to be able to be back together, to hang out again, be friends again and love each other without having to hide it all.

In October Granny Jean and I planned a Harvest party for the building. Jay and I flirted all night, sharing our food. Some people near us watched and smiled. Then we were all discussing ideas for the Christmas Party. Fred had gone to this dinner where you changed tables sampling items from different ethnic groups. People started listing the different ethnic groups represented by those living in the building. Jason pops up and says, "Rose is kinda sweetish."

You could have heard a pin drop I swear. Everyone got quiet and just looked at us. They had watched us flirt all night, knew we were together so why did it shock them so much? Perhaps they didn't realize he was as much in love with me as I was him, or just believed all the rumors going around. Who knows?

One night Fred took Jason and me out to this new Mexican restaurant/bar in Ripon. The food was great and we had a good time. Jason drove Fred's truck back to the building because Fred had had a few drinks. Fred doesn't like anyone driving his baby as he calls it, so to let Jason was a big deal.

We walked over to another bar/restaurant just up the street from the building. Fred and Jason played pool as I watched. Jason is actually a good player and it was fun to watch him. Then Fred got into flirting with the female bartender so Jason and I played some music on the jukebox and danced. We didn't care what people thought, if they watched us. We were having a good time. It got late and Jason and I said goodnight to Fred and walked back home. Jason had to get up to go to work the next morning.

Well one of the biggest busybodies in the building who started all these rumors about me and had helped get Abbie to break me and Jason up, must have seen us go out that night and didn't like it. She must have either called Abbie herself or had someone else do it, because Abbie started calling Jason again all the time, several times a day in fact and hounding him at work. She asked him to go here or there with her. He told me about it.

I tried to handle it right. I wasn't going to tell him what to do. He knew what she had done to him, how she had made him feel. He was the one who had to handle it and tell her no. Though I tried to make it clear that I didn't like her calling him and putting the pressure on again.

Turns out Abbie also had the guys at work bullying him to go back out with her. The pressure he was under before was nothing compared to the pressure put on him this time. He should have been honest with me, with them all, and we could have dealt with it together. But he didn't tell me about the pressure he was under. I found out later after Abbie succeeded in breaking us up again.

One night I was hanging with Jason at his place. He had just given me this great backrub. We kissed a little and he told me that I was the best girlfriend that he had ever had. Then he told me I had to go because someone was coming over at 9. He told me that Abbie was coming over after work, taking a taxi, (since she had crashed two cars and hadn't yet gotten a new one her parents were driving her back and forth to work) and was going to stay the night so she could ride with him to work in the morning.

I didn't like it. I didn't like it one bit. I knew what she was trying to do and he was going to let her, again. "She better not sleep in your bed," I told him.

"I will sleep on the couch," Jason replied.

"I trust you," I told him. "But I do not trust her."

"She won't be sexy anyways all messy from work."

What the fuck! Why would he say something like that? Here he had me on his couch half undressed for the backrub, says I am the best girlfriend he ever had and is blowing me off to let some other female spend the night. He said he didn't want to have sex with me because she was coming over. Knowing what she had done to him before, was just manipulating him. It didn't make any sense. Of course after I found out later about the pressure he was under it made more sense, some, but it still wasn't right.

As I expected Jason came over the next day after work to talk to me. "I'm going to date Abbie."

"What about me?" I asked. I didn't want to but I started to cry. Last time I didn't let him see my tears. This time why should I hide them? He wrapped his arms around me and held me.

"We can be best friends," he replied.

"We have tried that before, several times. It didn't work because there is more between us than that," I told him.

"I know. If you were rich I'd marry you." Strange thing to say I thought.

"Oh, only if I was rich?" I teased, smiling with my cheeks wet from tears. "Well when my books start selling I may be rich."

"No, I'd marry you anyways. I love you." Then why? This makes no sense. I was getting very confused.

"So what is it that you want to do? Not what she wants you to do, but what you want?" I asked him.

"I want to date her." By the look on his face and the change in the tone of his voice I knew he was lying. He was definitely lying.

"You love me. Want to marry me one day. Yet you want to date her. That makes no sense." I told him.

"No it doesn't. I don't understand it either." He said.

Then he left. I was left confused, hurt, all matter of emotions running through me. What was going on? How could he love me and yet be with her? Again the answer lies in the pressure he was under and the fact that he never learned to stand up for himself.

Needless to say we weren't allowed to be best friends, or any kind of friends. Every time we would even talk to each other Abbie would pull the chain she had on him tighter. She could see how Jason and I felt about each other. She could hear it in his voice as he talked to me when she was with him, how he ignored her when he was talking to me. She loved it when I got upset when she was there. When I would cry or get real mad and slam a door. Our misery was her pleasure.

Yet our love continued even in chaos. A true treasure for us both to keep and hold. The story is not over. New chapters will be written as months and years pass. How long Jason and I will continue to be in each others chapters I do not know. Who can? But love is eternal even if two people are torn apart.

The greatest treasure though that I have found throughout all this, these relationships and my healing journey, is to love myself. That is the beginning. I could not love Jason until I loved me. Abuse robs you of all that, those positive feelings of self you develop as you learn and grow in childhood.

It was a long hard climb, but I made it. There are plenty more mountains to climb and valleys filled with dark and terrible things. I made it through the beginning, which is the hardest part. Those first steps, learning how to deal with things no one should ever have to deal with, trying to find some idea of who you are and what you want and need. I made it through. So I will make it through the rest too.

Inside us all is a true treasure waiting to be discovered. No matter how happy your past or how horrid you can still find yourself lost. A stranger looking back at you in the mirror. Problems and stresses can rob you, make you hide within, pretend all is okay when it isn't. We are all under pressure to be something other than who we are, the person we are deep down inside.

God created us all unique for a reason. Even identical twins have some differences in at least personality and how they respond to things around them. Find your uniqueness. Be it. Love yourself, despite mistakes, despite problems, despite illnesses. Love yourself. That is the greatest treasure from which all the rest flows to touch the world with light.

FOOTNOTE

My name is Fenix. I am one of Rose's "Alternative Personalities" or Alters. I was born when Rose was 8 years old. I wanted to write a footnote for this book.

Rose is a unique individual. With all she has been through she does not hate. Does not bear any grudges. She sees things differently than most people do. She sees through all the masks and lies and pretense people hide behind to the truth of who they are, the truth behind their behaviors. It would irritate me at times when she tried to help me see the same things, when all I wanted to do was be angry, to hate. Rose is right of course. Her way makes her a better person, makes us all in the Rose Garden better people, makes some of the people around her better people.

Some people however, hate her for being as she is. They use her being multiple as an excuse. Accuse her of faking it all for attention, that DID isn't real. Accuse her of a lot of things. Some did it because she saw the truth about them and they didn't like it. Everyone else they could snow, but not Rose. Others did it because they liked being miserable, blaming others for their problems and well, Rose just by being herself with her compassion and understanding of things inspired people, encouraged, comforted.

Rose stopped growing at 13 because of something that happened that one summer. It was just one to many traumas in a life full of trauma. I know she describes the day she stopped living in one of the chapters, so I need not. Rose went through the motions, but a lot of it was done by one of us. She was never alone though she did not know it. She was not aware of how we helped her get through each day, go to school, to work, interact with people.

She didn't flirt or tease. She dressed to hide in baggy clothes. Even kept her weight up as another way to hide, to protect herself. So she never dated. She never believed she would be loved, could be loved and so had given up on life. She lived to help others, that was all.

As all of us started coming out and her past started to be revealed, not only did her body start changing, but there were all these behaviors of ours coming out. Behaviors that Rose just wasn't used to and didn't fit the image she had of herself.

Cera, born at 16, was the one who fell in love with Jake. That was very hard on Rose, believing what she did about herself, believing the lies that had been in place so long she didn' t even know they were lies. I know in this book Rose had to write in the first person or else it would have been very confusing. But those were Cera's feelings not Rose's. Cera was the one hurt by Jake that night and it broke her, changed her.

Rose had never been in love. Though she had shown love to so many people in so many ways, no one had ever really loved her and she had never really loved anyone. She was closed off from life, while helping others to live. That is until the day she met Jason.

Jason was the first, the only guy Rose ever responded to in a good way. Before then any male who hit on her made her very uncomfortable, even literally sick. From that day Rose started coming alive, but she wasn't aware of it. She started growing, changing. She thought it was the Triplets, hid behind them, as one of them was always with her when she was out, except when she was with Jason. Rose was in love and didn't realize it. Couldn't believe it was her, that her life wasn't over, but just beginning, afraid to believe it. Jason fell in love with her too. Finally after all the Hell Rose had been through, a piece of Heaven.

But as in all stories of true love there are those who fight against it. People consumed with jealousy, prejudice, hate who will do whatever they can to cause trouble, to separate the lovers. Little rumors when Jason and Rose started dating, that could be laughed off or ignored. Outright hatred and harassment, threats when Rose refused to break up with Jason when he had his breakdown. Slander that got so bad Rose was afraid to leave our apartment. Jason was being harassed too. Why his "inner protector" came out and dated some other girl, one these people wanted him to be with, would accept, hoping that things would settle down and Rose and Jason would be left alone. But that isn't what happened.

Things didn't settle down. The tongues never stopped wagging, but got worse, more vicious. In February of 2007, well it was so bad that four of us died. The Triplets (Cera, Red, Dianah) and Hannah, who was only 14. They also loved Jason and some of his alters, were involved with them themselves. One night the four of them said goodbye to us and walked out into the woods around the cabin, our safe house, then into the darkness and died.

Some don't believe that they are dead. They say that Alters can't die. They must just be hiding. Because we don't have four bodies buried in four graves with four headstones it isn't real to them. It is real to us. Very real to Rose. She lost her stabilizers. The ones who helped her go shopping, socialize, everything. It was hard on all of us loosing our sisters, but hardest on her. She didn't know what she would do, how she would handle things. We worried too about what would happen to us.

It was after that though, that terrible thing, that Rose saw that she had changed, grown, was alive and no longer in the backseat watching everything. That was because of her relationship with Jason, because of their love. Their love that brought out the worst in some people and caused our sisters death. They were murdered by forked poisoned tongues.

These people still won't leave Rose alone. Just a few people, three or four who are doing this. Who others know are doing it, who themselves hear and see it, but won't say anything, do anything. Most people see Rose as sweet and kind and helpful. An angel as Rosie Lo calls her. I don't understand why these few hate her so much. Why they think they have the right to do what they are doing.

I am the angry one so I get very pissed off and swear and yell and play music real loud and take it out on video or computer games. I wish I could fight. I wish I could go right up to them and tell them off. But I don't. I can't. It wouldn't do no good. These people have permission from the silence of the others around us to do this to Rose. People know and don't care because it isn't their life. It isn't them being harassed. As long as they are left alone then it is okay. Even if it means they can't talk to Rose, be neighborly with her. Even if it means watching her be broken again and again and Jason along with her.

Rose has a heart full of light and love, like few people have. A gift of understanding and compassion and wisdom that goes way beyond her years, her experience. She has been exposed to the worst a human being can be and do to an innocent and yet doesn't hate, only loves. She is the true treasure. One the rest of us in this Rose Garden were born to protect. One that this world desperately needs.